Hinge &

McHugh,
1948-
   Hinge & sign

W

Heather McHugh

Hinge  Sign

Poems, 1968–1993

WESLEYAN UNIVERSITY PRESS
Middletown, Connecticut

Published by Wesleyan University Press, Middletown, CT 06459
Printed in the United States of America 10 9 8 7 6 5 4
CIP data appear at the end of the book

*Originally produced in 1994 by Wesleyan/University Press of New England,
Hanover, NH 03755*

Acknowledgments appear on page 217

For Niko

Contents

Poems from A World of Difference (1977–1981) 121

Poems from To the Quick *(1981–1987)*   151

Poems from Shades *(1981–1988)*   181

Preface

Soy un fue, y un sera, y un es cansado.
[I am a was, and a will be, and a tired is.]
—Francisco de Quevedo (1580–1645)

This offering of new poems, together with selections from my
past books, comprising some twenty-five years in all, was not so
much a labor of love (only the newest-hatched work still bears in
relation to its creator sufficient strangeness to be lovable) as it was
a work of wariness. For one thing, despite the reassurances of
friends and editors, I was subject to the persistent suspicion that
all lecteds (se- no less than col-) are more or less directly prepost-
humous. For another, I was subject to the subject, and I didn't
always like her.

The -lecteds remind us, etymologically, not of their status as
writings but rather of their status as readings; and, certainly, to
have gone back over decades of the writing of someone I no
longer *am* is to have been engaged in a strange kind of reading:
one in which I am doubly implicated. (Somebody—Chester-
ton?—said that autocriticism does honor to the writer, dishonor
to the critic.) Even given the greatest scrupulousness as to self-
regard, there are persistent parallaxes, skews of space and time.

But writing, like reading, implies in any case a very peculiar
form of presence. It is presence at *another* moment. In this anach-
ronism, this unsettled time, the intimacy between writer and
reader (unlike other intimacies) seems the closer for its definition
in deferral. Taking up any book to read it, how am I *with* the
writer? This *with* is without the usual conversational confronting;
for I identify myself as (I don't identify myself over against) the
unfolding. I am *with* the writer not *en face*, as an opposite respon-
dent, but *à tête*, as a kind of mind-reader.

And as a writer, how am I with the reader? This is an engage-
ment with a very non-particular someone, an other very like a
self, unseeable, a grounding figure which, when I do take the
trouble to imagine it (for one need not *imagine* a being to *have*
one), I imagine as a fellow-imaginer: as an understanding—even
an underwriting—inmate. Any engagement in acts of reading,
between that figure and myself, is engagement without argument,
engagement without preliminaries, engagement without (in any
of the usual senses) even a meeting of minds: there was never,

after all, a separation. To be a writer "with" a reader is rather like being, oneself, of two minds, at every turn: hinge and sign. By comparison with this intimacy, the fondest act of physical love takes place between strangers.

The writing of poems is, itself, always a kind of reading, but reading under the pressures of presence: all one knows of past and portent bears in on the writing, and becomes *of moment*: one second, three disappearances (in tense as in person). A pier appears, a bridge built to land nowhere but in structure's end itself, in wavering. A rocking, a consolidated light; we get bright wet, and nowhere fast.

Sometimes you *can* judge a book by its cover. In the photograph on this collection of poems I hoped to catch that moment in which figure is hard to tell from ground (the earth we're made of, the humus the human's rooted in). In this view, layering and shades of ground gave the figures depth (instead of the other way around). A human figure is a hinged sign anyway, but two together make another set of signs and hinges: doubling up like quotation marks, resembling, dissembling, assembling. For even the loneliest soul alive, it takes two.

One is, already, a convocation (of times, of beings). Writing is the thick and thin one goes through with such times of being, with such beings of time. I is an other, says Rimbaud. (You might think, in this citation, *is* says it all. But maybe, with regard to the poet's presence, *says* says it all. Beckett raises a cautionary eyebrow here, as we go down the sway-ways of saying: "Whenever said said said missaid." I love Beckett for his wealth of alternative, his want of comma.)

One is undone, in any case. (In French, one is *un*.) And *nom*, after all, is all but *non*. Speech is parts; is isn't. If there's an all at all, it seems to me a rushing, a curving, a swaying I'm supposed (by something higher-up) to hold (in mind, in line). The sign moves by virtue of the hidden hinge; the poem signs, sighs, sings of meaning made moving. I don't know any better way for words than poems, to hold these sways. A poem contains meaning only the way a body contains life: moving, it IS it.

Writing has always been in me the site not of an intention, but of an intensity. Eudora Welty, asked if she didn't believe that universities stifled writers, answered "Not enough of them." If I could keep from words, I would. I can't make highfalutin claims for my broken silence, though I suppose I have a gift for listening to language before I make it listen to me; it's a habit of resisting habit, and keeps me (as I grow older and more patient) from some of the more presumptuous familiarities. As a daily aesthetic, it goes beyond rhetorical exercise: the main discipline is to keep finding life strange (this is the extent, and intent, of spirituality in me). Tongue-tied, tongue-twisted, tongue-lashed, who wouldn't admire those venerable monks able to say an eloquent nothing for merciful months—who liberate years from their yammering, deliver decades from their dicta?

At eighteen, I was bored and begloomed by *Watt*; now, a quarter of a century later, how utterly it's changed! (You cannot read the same book twice, I read once.) These three decades have reBecketted me, three decades as a human being driven (read: given) to write. To my ear now, less brass, more irony, his work, scored for intellect and experience, seems slappingly tonic. Even his most obsessive streaks (madnesses of permutation) rise to occasions of haunting, hilarious economy (the axis of excess can change, in a flash of ghost or laughter). When Beckett spins his wheels, even the mud is funny.

As the world's shyest child, I was the one who never spoke in school but who registered, with uncalled-for intensity, every twist of tone and talk; who, at home, went directly to her room to write, because writing proposed a fellow-listener, though things seemed quite unspeakable. This present collection, retrospective, keeps for its true (if hidden) title a word I lift, heartstrung, to—and from—the Beckett it took me all these years to understand: it's *ununsaid.*

after Rilke

Closed up like a mouth after a cry
the white house has its blinds all drawn.
Out on the sundial, a peacock lies,
causing mid-day hours to be gone.

The roses will lose themselves tonight,
too full of petalling, in gentle agonies.
My child, my friend, do not refuse the sight:
for death gives life its clarities.

New Poems

1987–1993

What He Thought

for Fabbio Doplicher

We were supposed to do a job in Italy
and, full of our feeling for
ourselves (our sense of being
Poets from America) we went
from Rome to Fano, met
the mayor, mulled
a couple matters over (what's
cheap date, they asked us; what's
flat drink). Among Italian literati

we could recognize our counterparts:
the academic, the apologist,
the arrogant, the amorous,
the brazen and the glib—and there was one

administrator (the conservative), in suit
of regulation gray, who like a good tour guide
with measured pace and uninflected tone narrated
sights and histories the hired van hauled us past.
Of all, he was most politic and least poetic,
so it seemed. Our last few days in Rome
(when all but three of the New World Bards had flown)
I found a book of poems this
unprepossessing one had written: it was there
in the *pensione* room (a room he'd recommended)
where it must have been abandoned by
the German visitor (was there a bus of *them?*)
to whom he had inscribed and dated it a month before.
I couldn't read Italian, either, so I put the book
back into the wardrobe's dark. We last Americans

were due to leave tomorrow. For our parting evening then
our host chose something in a family restaurant, and there
we sat and chatted, sat and chewed,
till, sensible it was our last
big chance to be poetic, make
our mark, one of us asked
                    "What's poetry?

Is it the fruits and vegetables and
marketplace of Campo dei Fiori, or
the statue there?" Because I was

the glib one, I identified the answer
instantly, I didn't have to think—"The truth
is both, it's both," I blurted out. But that
was easy. That was easiest to say. What followed
taught me something about difficulty,
for our underestimated host spoke out,
all of a sudden, with a rising passion, and he said:

The statue represents Giordano Bruno,
brought to be burned in the public square
because of his offense against
authority, which is to say
the Church. His crime was his belief
the universe does not revolve around
the human being: God is no
fixed point or central government, but rather is
poured in waves through all things. All things
move. "If God is not the soul itself, He is
the soul of the soul of the world." Such was
his heresy. The day they brought him
forth to die, they feared he might
incite the crowd (the man was famous
for his eloquence). And so his captors
placed upon his face
an iron mask, in which

he could not speak. That's
how they burned him. That is how
he died: without a word, in front
of everyone.   And poetry—
                                        (we'd all
put down our forks by now, to listen to
the man in gray; he went on
softly)—
                        poetry is what

he thought, but did not say.

Acts of God

I. Tornado

I said the people come inside.
They would be safe
in the building.
So many of those people die.
You can see my guilt.

I could see hands
to a lady moving.
I knew the lady.
You can see my guilt.

Sometimes I want to run, to get
away from it. I ask forgiveness
night and day, I ask it from
the cemetery. I can never
dream this storm away.

It was over for maybe minutes
then it was never over.

II. Lightning

It pushed me backward, I could see
my friends go backward, too,
as from a blast, but slowly,
very slowly, everything was in
a different time.

It burned inside my body.
I could feel my hands
curl up. My pocket got
on fire, I didn't want
to reach in there and take
a handful of the hot.
My money hurt.

I'm different now forever, put that fact
into your book. My hair used to be straight.
My eyes—you see? They're gray as ash.
They used to be light blue. You live,

if you're lucky, but take my word—

it changes how you look.

Window: Thing as Participle

Welling and flowing and fastening, too,
the window itself became the fever,
faces waved and surfed
across its surface . . .

Stop that, she rebuked herself,
people are only passing on the sidewalk,
people are simply walking on the sidepass, yes,
that's all you're seeing, so much

water in an eye. But then the sneezes rose
from somewhere to attack
whole buildings, schools and churches,
massive stoneworks, city hall—
whatever stood, stood to be wracked—
did no one notice? They were all
at risk: whatever the window held
could tremble. Mortified, she sat

in the eye of the storm, with steam
from cups of cure to drape
or dramatize her time away; but still
the window went on streaming
all these bundled half-lives by, in one
continuous unravelling of differences, of
higher, lower, lighter, darker,
faces framed in fur or bared of head,
blown blond or blasted black, each one appointed
in a halo's freeze-burn or an aura's sun-chill,
each one with its hunch of forehead, over
only two hot coals per person . . .

Humankind was understandable in this
unending sentence of an EEG she witnessed
scrolling by; it was, at each new moment, modelled
into spikes of single-mindedness; but every
bobbing of discreteness in the flow, each
block or chunk, each head, she knew
(she knew) had its

own helixing and coils
of orienting endlessness, its moving
windows of reflective flux,
and its own someone
in a fix: that figure
underlying everything, that glimpse

in brown or blue, with fringe of lash:
a holy icon, prize of self, an image
irrecoverably, shimmeringly
still, it is so deeply

plunged into the nominative . . .

Curve

Freezeburn forms whirlpools and bearfur has curve.
My line is gravity's
sheer vertical.

Memory's the same
seme. Sail a memo
down: there's the spooled

real: plunge into simul-
cast. Caught up in the network is
a blue planet, spinner par
excellence.

It's too small.
Throw it back.

Dry Time

Killed, the sand
didn't give. All waves
went dead: your border
crossed itself.

I couldn't tell or tear
us apart. In the absence
of hourglasses
meanwhiles

piled up, swells of the
dispellable. Even the diamond
shed no oil, not a drop
to delight the drilltip.

    *

Partners having come
unwelded (blasted by nuclear
family life) we went
a long

way back,
as far as Abacus (empire of
the rook and stork). We roused
some dowsers

from a timeless doze, we had them
scatter Onan's
nanoseconds
everywhere: in waves and particles, the clearest

solitudes could be
broadcast. At last
you kissed me, I
could die again, and one

good lick
of quick-
sand took . . .

Seal

Born flipper-first into an icy wind
it gropes to locate anything hospitable, and that
turns out to be a nipple, cuffed in fur.
It has to live the next few months

upon that knowledge, and a frozen shelf.

In time the nipple-bearer pulls away, into a sensible
give-and-take; becomes a moving meaning.
Then in time it's plain
the white world has
an edge. Familiars disappear across it,

reappear with hides ashine. The waddler
noses toward, along, and half across
the terrifying line. At last the most
reluctant selfhood dares

to plunge,

out of the known and
over the border and
down. And there,
beneath his native ground—

lo and behold—
another world, a world
of milder currencies, inverted
cumulus and azure, verticals and shade,
the velvets of a deep interior and turns

of coy comestibility—

in short, another life,
with footholds made
for memory. (In this
expanded universe, the sky

is naturally

surmountable—but why?
Why lumber clumsily, above it all—
if able in an underworld to fly?)

Two-Legged

Man is A
and woman's
B. The rut is deep
because of cause.
The bull
is hooked
not avid.
Some where some
narrator's lettered:
fest of nails, be-
quest of feed:
a real mail habit.

*

Her suede hold, this dancer's,
minds me to ax
the aesthete what he mean, next time
I see him. Opposites at

racked removes: trees bloodlines,
fingers thumb, swirl of brush its aftershot whirlpools:
DNA its fine ID. Yes no, saw was.

Shouldest its own real quest.

*

Hand to mouth, you weight, equate, and are
the agent. Planted most
means move. (And weirdest, yes, of all
first persons is

the priest in his
two-legged pants.)
God's Zed.

Fast

I love a rock, for holding
so much down (itself, for example,
its grounds). From where we stand it seems

to set loose Alps of cloud above;
below, the lilies range
around its late, light-catching

faces. Lawns run right up to
its settledness: Your
Highness! buzz the grasses and

Your Heaviness! (their blades
ablaze). For they must come
and go, attracted now

to this, now that, while it
is always going—going with
the monolithic given,

given every day to love
(in winter as in heat)
only the planet's plunge through heaven.

Coming

is the body's way
of weeping, after a series
of shocks is suffered, after the thrust
of things, the gist of things, becomes
apparent: the bolt is felt completely
swollen in vicinity to wrench,
the skid is clearly headed
toward an all-out insult, and the senses
one by one abandon all their stations—
into smaller hours and thinner
minutes, seconds
split—till POW—

you had it, had it coming, and it heaved, whose participle
wasn't heaven.
That
was that.
And when you got

some senses back,
you asked yourself, is this
a dignified being's way
of being born? What
a thought
somebody had! (or some no-body)

out of the breathless blue, making us
double up like this, half gifted and
half robbed. "Rise up to me," the spirit

laughed. "I'm
coming, I'm coming,"
the body sobbed.

Glimpse of Main Event

In the slump between rounds he looks
older. He's been living
fast. Some water glances off him,
nicks of glitter.

Time having stopped a while,
he droops on his stool.
In the foreground a female
torso carves

a curve of sequins past him, expunging
his face for a second.
Before and after her
the trainer's visible, looking

down and in, urgent
with his Adam.
Scales flicker, in that fray of moments,
in the eye of the beholder.

My Shepherd

A name's another thing
in dog-dom. Fido the Uberpooch is dead,
some singing's overcome the underhund.

The underhund's no private
nose or eye. Smells well, sights bound.
He cops his swill from the bar's back door,
scopes kibble out in big denominations;
even his birthday suit
is finest furs; you'll have
no other dog before me, he rebarks; I'll be
boygone. I'll be

downhome, awaiting his arrival.
What I mean by home is
totally upgussied: I've
got five pink weenies in the microwave
(he loves paw-long hot-men); I've licked
the floorboards spick, the chain-link span.
I've almost utterly forgotten
any other master (man:

the heaviest
of absentees, you do
the gorge-tattoo, the choke-a-throat. To you

we're Fidos or we're Rovers;
deep in mastery of mind there is

no other kind.) Thank Dog our star
is no cartoon—it's Sirius, not Pluto,
and the one I'm waiting for
won't call me by
my human name. He'll lift

a leg to the polestar, he'll
speak bone; he'll bow and
wow me, nose the moistened

meat. He knows the sweetest
senses of the shady. In the end,

because he cannot lie,

he'll switch me back to Bitch,
from Lady.

Untitled

There is much unsaid, though the edges of the said
so long and so
perversely have
attracted me. And even now
how can I tell
what old unbearabilities of mind in animal amount

to my drive to seize you, you who have
become my being's being,
owner than myself? Parmenides' muse
(Dike the indicator, Dike the just)
insists no part is more existent
than another, no part less; and yet

there SEEMS to be less being in a self
than in another: self is least
the seeable, in self's esteem; one's sense of it
a sixth, at most, whereas one's senses of another
billow full and five . . . YOU I can feel

all ways: I run an eye on your leg,
look a foot in your eye. In you
I am very advanced: I see the end
of my own inwardness. But if I turn

to me, the second splits. There's instantaneous
adjustment—surface slid in place: I face someone who's always
facing back, or inside-out, or rightside-down;

someone who saw me first, and fixed herself;
someone whose other faces I know nothing of.
If for a moment she were clearly
visible to me, I think

I'd fall forever, out of love.

The Woman Who Laughed on Calvary

I.

Smilers, smirkers, chucklers, grinners,
platitudinizers, euphemists: it wasn't you

I emulated there, in that
Godawful place. What kind
of face

to put on it? How simple
is a simon's sign? To my mind
laughter's not the mark of pleasure, not
a pleasantry that spread; instead

it's intimate with sheer
delirium: spilt brain
on split lip, uncontainable
interiority—
(make no mistake, it *is* a horror, this

inmated, intimated
self, revealed as your
material: red smear,
white swipe). It's said the brain
stinks first, then organworks of art and eatery,
and then—what's left? a little cartilage for

ambiguity? a little tendon's B&D? At last, the least
ephemeral of evidences: nuggetworks (discrete, and
indiscreet) of teeth, bone-bits, odd scraps
of a delapidated strut—and this is just
the sort of stuff, insensate,
to which life (which comes again

as slime) has always
loved adhering. Life! Who wouldn't
laugh? Your inner life! Your pet
pretense! It can't be kept up, can't
be kept clean,
even in a thought,

except a good
bloodworks or shitpump keeps it so.

II.

Out of the mouth comes a tongue,
it calls itself linguistic and it
never quite effects
the cover-up (good
Lord, there's much to
cover up: so many belches, outcries,
upchucks, sneezes, puffings, hiccups, osculations, hawks and
　coughs)—

so laughter (which, among the noises, prides itself
on being the most intellectual) can't help
but come out, snorting. Nothing

smiled or mild or meanwhiling—a laugh's
got teeth to send it off,
and spit to keep it company, and rot
to end up with. Its closest kin is grimace, it's
a grimacing with wind.
It will (the will
be damned)
burst out

in bad cacaphonies of
brouhaha and borborygma—it's the
stockbroker of mockeries, a trachea rake—
the vent of rage and irony, and right
there in the very
shrine of signs. A laugh, I mean,
is sorrow's

archery and signature,
while flesh is being
hoisted and arrayed

on roosts of skeleton.

III.

I saw what good

comes to; I saw the figure

human being cuts, upon its frame.
The laugh was a cry from my own

perscrewed, misnailed, cross-crafted
armature. Despite

your consternations, oh you
meekened warners and polite
conventioneers, the thieves were better
served upon that day. For the heart

is a muscle, where cruelty's humored.
The tooth of moral rectitude's
a fang. What I gave

at the sight of him there

was up. What I got
of humanity there
was the hang . . .

Eastport

I drove a day and a night
over poured concrete, over moon
macadams, now and then corrected
by an intermittent dashing; I

turned right at the first
fierce sign, and went
till I hit wet. The wet
was only starting, so I stopped.

The night passed not
as time but space, and pushed
sunshine, and then the sun itself, from up the other
side of islands. When I woke the world had turned

into a neighborhood
of new-cropped rock, and one
whole nowhere of sea-smoke,
adrift as if alive.

Well

I swear affective life is water:
variously formed and regulated,
curiously colored and abounded,
but at heart
always the same
wet element. And we

are made of it.

No single thing, or unremitting motion,
it can fall (as joy) in flashes
from high rocks, in sprays
of spectra (by its virtue,
sun can be broadcast); or rise

as sorrow, once and for all,
to muddy the living room, rob
the lover of her breathing space . . . Sometimes

its affect is half-bred: a trickle on
a cobblestone, a swamp with flesh-colored
flowers in it,
ice from an eave . . . What

ranges of ringing,
of whooshing and whisking it makes.
Inside our heads (the experts say) there's
nonstop noise: what we call
silence, it's our grounds for sound . . .

Maybe it's water, what broke
so we'd be born; maybe it bore

and goes on bearing us,
till humankind and animals and
gods themselves are swept up
in its school of thought,

till the exploding stars are only
quiet points, afloat. I tell you, even

anaesthesia's a feeling.
(It's the feeling we forgot.)

Unguent

Instead of angels, give us aero-
gels. Diaphanous as surfaces of soap,

lightest of the solids on this earth,
an aerogel won't burn, beneath our most
insistent blowtorch. We created it to be
a lightweight indestructibility,
just as we did (in good
old days) our bombs, and just
as in the good old days, we'll sell
a bit of it to you. Just take

our word for it, it's better
than the gist of gism, better than the best
of bed. Directly out of it will come
the aero-arrows of idea, which lead
to speech balloons and quick ignition pens.
Between the coupled wars, and times, and causes, prime
seems fed up, misled, laid. A thought

is nothing but a need
for energy, a body's mission: be
suggestive to a head. Instead of angels,

give us urges. We'll take over, if the mover's dead.

Some Kind of Pine

Mid-leap in her escape, the nymph
is bushed: one hand bursts out in

branches, tropes turn
helio. The hapless god

has suffered some comeuppance, too:
he's stuck for good in his own stalking.

The maker's a remarker, casting animal as vegetable and then
their motions turn to mineral, their moments into monument.

*

So now the downcast god puts forth forever
in the Villa's living-room

preposterous, unsinkable, his best
foremember. There it is, a figurative branching toward

her laurel literality. She can't, in time,
escape; he can't, in time, arrive.

They're caught for good in this
ambiguous ambition:

one extending, one intending,
never to be free.

*

Right now, as I write "now,"
one happenstance of courtyard tree appears
attractively more literal than theirs (as yours,
if you have one, must seem to you

more literal than mine—by mine, I mean this actual and un-
possessible mid-summer something . . . what's its name, this

evergreen—beyond the hotel balcony whose French doors—do
   they
call them that, in Italy?—I flung wide open to escape

*

my rectitude of narrow-bedded room). The conifers outside confer
a ringing down on everything; and water whooshes

white around a bend; the branches
glimmer at the tips. (Are they

some kind of pine?) I'm moved
by them, now that I've come

to rest, from so many thousands of
words (numbed space, named time). I stand

*

at planet-speed, struck dumb
before such patiences as these, that surge for years to crown

in great calm altitudes, in starful prongs. How did they get
so far? They leave us to our babbling, they ignore

the running reasons of the human stream; they pour
into the sky. That's what they're standing for:

for standing fast. They are a sign
we shall not overcome, except

in undergoing more . . .

Numberless

. . . composed that monstrous animal, a husband and wife.—Henry Fielding

By law of rod and cone, the closer
it gets, the darker it looks. We look
benighted. I can hardly make out
elbow, lobe or nape, and once we go
into the whole conundrum, it's by blind
feel, slowly summing something's curve, or
multiplying verbs to come, toward where

our things have gone—the lampshade, doorknob, chair—
    they've
gone inside: they've faded into
eyelid, nipple, hip;
it isn't long
before the room
and roof, the world at large is gone
inside us, into humming, thumping, damp, and then
there's only inside left to lose, and then it too
is lost, all's
lost, in a
drench, a
din of downfall . . .

(Voltage pours away in brilliant

paralyzing pulse . . .)

*

Four walls and seven
windows reappear. Our shoes
show up, right where we left them.
Glasses poised beside the bed, the innocence
that led us into such an indistinction. Now
the eight-limbed animal begins
to pull apart, into

the two of us. There's ticking,
there's a cooling off. I see,

upon a pillow, seven
inches from my face,

the watched wrists fallen
side by side: and yours
is a remming of fast-asleep
silvers. The other must be mine:

it's wide awake, it's strapped with hide.

To Go

Quelle, et si fine, et si mortelle
que soit ta pointe . . . —Paul Valéry, *"L'Abeille"*

I don't know what bee balm is
and all those rose hips
dying to be used . . .
But when the backyard comes alive
in humming-season, blurred with wings,
and red wild jewelweed is dangling
dangerous attractions, hook over stalk, I know

I'll see, with long enough regard
(the kind you need to catch a meteor
across the crest of August)

soon or late the wicked

bee, flamboyant bee, the bee
of holy hellishness, about
to pick the pinkest
pocket of my backyard blaze. A single

point of tension, an attention, it
will light on the lower and outlapping
lip of a flower, follow the tonguehairs in to where
the sex-light lies . . . One bee exactly

fills a bee-sized bloom, and so one's urge
(with thumb and forefinger) is this: to close
the lips of it, about the bumbler's
art, and gently pull
the whole small
sac of
business
off the plant,
and have it there

in hand, one bee to go.

But why? Why so desire
to have and hold? Because
because because because. (Inside of

one life is another: it's our
nature, to be wanting a beyond,
somewhere for will to go on
growing out of was,
somewhere for never
to be next of kin to yet.)
The possibilities become us,
even in our sleep—the whirl

belongs to flesh, the humming
to electrons—being we could keep,
buzzes we could get.

Connubial

Dream's matterless, it dips
from bounds to billowings;

laws lapse in it,
and universes swerve.

Before I had
an other at my side

there was no side. (How far
can onesome go?) Just being

here at hand, just being, beating
in and out of phase, you are

my bounds and bearings: touch
is couch, about aflow.

    *

(Blind comfort, maybe, keeping
terrifying lights away . . . But one is one's
own zero, hole through which the all
can plunge appallingly. I'm not
cut out for it—not yet—
by mind and hand I'm given to

symmetrical identities, or
solitudes of two.) And if I've settled
for a circumstance (landings broken
by water, starfalls by blue)—

so be it. Loving's limited;
its singularity is all reprise.
You save me from, not for, eternities.

Prothalamion

Am I detached enough
to recognize (on its
own, if it were presented
to me bare, without its
rings about or wiring to
Myself Incorporated)—this

odd thing, my mind-dog,
amanuensis, my
right hand?

Like its master the mind,
it's been on itself (on
hand, that is) forever.
It is all I have

to know it with. I feel

myself, a finger on
a palm; I try to grasp
which is the object: which
feels felt. Would I recognize

my hand displayed
on a platter (assuming sufficient
anaesthesia to lull
the arm and mind meanwhile)?
Would I identify
its thumb, my thumb—could I
identify *with* it? Wouldn't the rule

of thumb (foregone conclusion)
suddenly be broken—human rule, unsung,
of self-attachment? I live more certainly
in such foregoneness than in open
actuality, I fear. Ah me! Dear
me! Of all identities precisely it's

the most assumed. How well have I ever
loved or studied it? And what about me

could I give to you? My hand?—lines
learned by heart but not by eye (the eye
goes deeper); networks held

in scant regard. A hand was always
moreorless a metaphor for me—
a number, one
of two, one
of hundreds, to be given
a caption here and there,
a cursory shake, a courtesy cough. Head, heart
and having, all three, took my hand. It wasn't really

there for me, until they cut it off.

The Size of Spokane

The baby isn't cute. In fact he's
a homely little pale and headlong
stumbler. Still, he's one
of us—the human beings
stuck on flight 295 (Chicago to Spokane);
and when he passes my seat twice
at full tilt this then that direction,
I look down from Lethal Weapon 3 to see
just why. He's

running back and forth
across a sunblazed circle on
the carpet—something brilliant, fallen
from a porthole. So! it's light
amazing him, it's only light, despite
some three and one
half hundred
people, propped in rows
for him to wonder at; it's light
he can't get over, light he can't
investigate enough, however many
zones he runs across it,
flickering himself.

The umpteenth time
I see him coming, I've had
just about enough; but then
he notices me noticing and stops—
one fat hand on my armrest—to
inspect the oddities of me.

*

Some people cannot hear.
Some people cannot walk.
But everyone was
sunstruck once, and set adrift.
Have we forgotten how
astonishing this is? so practiced all our senses

we cannot imagine them? foreseen instead of seeing
all the all there is? Each spectral port,
each human eye

is shot through with a hole, and everything we know
goes in there, where it feeds a blaze. In a flash

the baby's old; Mel Gibson's hundredth comeback seems
less clever; all his chases and embraces
narrow down, while we
fly on (in our
plain radiance of vehicle)

toward what cannot stay small forever.

Auto

At first, the mobiles were for multitudes—
the horse was doubled, then redoubled;

way and station made for
social arts, within which

conversations, trains of thought,
held sway. Today

I drive morosely and alone, like half
a billion others, each

in a glassed-in,
speakered-up

contraption, each
with a brain she thinks

she can control (it goes off
on its own, on detours

now and then; it dreams of cable-
cars and smoking-cars and Volkses that can spill

unthinkable powers of ten in clownface) unlike this poor
hollowed-out sedation of sedan I pull

off the throughway, up to the pump
marked SELF, and fill.

Better or Worse

I.

Daily, the kindergarteners
passed my porch. I loved
their likeness and variety,
their selves in line like little
monosyllables, but huggable—
I wasn't meant

to grab them, ever,
up into actual besmooches or down
into grubbiest tumbles, my lot was not
to have them, in the flesh.
Was it better or worse to let
their lovability go by untouched, and just
watch over their river of ever-
inbraiding relations? I wouldn't
mother them or teach. We couldn't be
each other's others; maybe,
at removes, each other's each.

II.

Each toddler had a hand-hold on
a loop of rope, designed to haul
the whole school onward
in the sidewalk stream—
like pickerel through freshets,
at the pull of something else's will, the children
spun and bobbled, three years old and four
(or were they little drunken Buddhas,
buoyant, plump?). They looked
now to the right, now to the sky, and now
toward nothing (nothing was too small)—
they followed a thread of destination,
chain of command, order of actual rope that led

to what? Who knew?

For here and now in one child's eye there was a yellow truck,

and in another's was a burning star; but from my own
    perspective,
overhead, adult, where trucks and suns had lost their luster,
they were one whole baby-rush toward
a target, toward the law
of targets, fledge
in the wake of an arrowhead;

a bull's-eye bloomed, a red
eight-sided sign. What
did I wish them?
Nothing I foresaw.

Two St. Petersburgs

I. Russia
The statue turned
upon a chain; beneath its broken knees
were thirty feet of air. Under its sway
of handwide eye stood, ludicrous,
a pedestal with only
feet on top. And under that

ranged real but little people, tiny
uprightnesses, all
abruptly free. Freely they milled,
collectively buzzed. They
feuded over food, they fell
in love anew, had words anew, had different
differences than heretofore. The differences were free

to spread; an air of half-lights made
for deep misgivings in the minds
of brand-new sunshade salesmen . . .

II. Florida
The desk clerk's disposition is
professionally sunny. In the waterbed room I ask
to be tied up, but nicely; you know
nooses that release.

Detachment has apartments and
attachment has departments. We can order
long and cool, or quick and hot. Or quick
and cool or long and hot. But can we do

the longer haul together? Keep the living daylights
ever-loving? Kill the cough?
For broken is a place
where something gave; a joint's

a place where something moved.
And eloquent is just

a mess of hinge and sign: a MO where the TEL
is not yet fallen off . . .

White Mind and Roses

Nobody's (not Rilke's even, whose
shade doesn't sleep), they are all
their own (are they a they?—this
shameless abundance that grows

most in the whirlpools
of its smell, till the whole
rosebush was never green, and memory's a moving
ground, for famous white explosions, flashpoints of
tissue and powers to die). The blooming itself

is a kind of time, a summerful
of outburst, or collective noun; but the trained eye notes
what few could wish to emulate: the fate
of the individual, that quickest course
in explicated radiance. Each rose is both

the lover and the source of light, seizer and liberator of
the lunary zones in men. Having done its utmost by
inventing us, with our rose-loving eyes and noses—having
over-done it, wasted billions on an animal
that sees the flowerer but not the flow—

and having finally grown rich beyond
the registers of narrow rubric—then

the bloom begins to turn: subtly
at first, only
a hint of yellow
(barely betraying
selves to itself); then suddenly

there's brown all over,
petal upon leaf and leaf upon
the stinging wood (once fraught
with whitest pyrotechnic, now
ubiquitously dark, it's

no less rose). Was it the whole we were
so busily admiring, when we missed

the sharp particulars (the hurtful ones,
the quick)? The whole has its
own bed and bud
and root and rot, and they
went unremarked as well (how much goes on
beneath our notice, being being
what it is). It's hard to tell. The darks exist

that could undo our ignorance, as days undid
our sense (sense in the singular,
that *idée fixe* whose urge is mainly to OUTdo
the other, shifting five) . . . But can a dark

undo our dread? When we're asleep is there
a murderer at large? What passes
all day for our ghost, at night
is it otherwise? Inside is it red?

Scenes from a Death

I wrapped my face in my cloak and wept for myself.—Plato

*

The women had been sent away so there would be no scenes,
but when their friend had actually drunk the cup of poison
then the men broke down like women and they wept.

*

The death of earth is to become water
and the death of water is to become air
and the death of air is to become fire
and reversely, Heraclitus says. I say
the death of us
is to become.

*

A plane appeared in the water
and a sail in the air,
the lichen on the crag was a gold
version of the greens you could see
upright in the oncoming sea; the tide
was timed just right and in our eyes
the brown and blue things bloomed.

*

The universe is transformation,
says the Stoic, in a mystic
moment. Life is only
an opinion. It's
philosophy he loves, not
poetry (which he adjudges
ornamental). What he does deem necessary, though,
is just exactly what I'd swear a poet does:
"make for yourself
a definition or description
of the thing which is presented you,
so as to see distinctly
what kind of thing it is
in its substance, in its nudity,

in its completeness; tell yourself
its proper name, and the names
of the things of which it's been compounded
and the others into which it will resolve . . .
Look at things so as to see
what kind of universe this is . . ."

     *

The day somebody dies you want
never to go to sleep. You want the day
in which he was alive
never to end.

Does darkness fall?
Or does the moviehouse of our mentality
just open, and its sense of inside
spread? Doesn't darkness escape from us,

to comprehend
the world as a whole—(take it,
or leave it, in other words, so we
can fall asleep)? Some weird bird

worried the dormant EEG, small hours
in the skullery. The darkness rose,
it didn't fall, to keep us all in mind,
where we can't tell branch from branch,

or time from time. But dot by dot
we needle our way back into the sky:
we reconstruct the (count 'em) eighty-eight
constellatory big ideas: starring

animals first, and then a hunter (whose weaponry
sparkles); then the mind bends down to its abode and puts
a chained woman near a winged horse. Now we have
a story again! One we can live under. Because lines

lead to points. Because points lead to lines. We thought
the big was strong, the little weak. But couldn't stop
the bird from screaming, or the night from shaking
in that brainstorm's beak . . .

*

The women had been sent away so there would be no scenes.
But when their friend had actually drunk the cup of poison
then the men broke down like women and they wept.

*

It rains all day and small birds tremble
in the cliff-side tree we call
a mountain ash (its leaves are feathery
as iron filings, radiant around a field of force).
The birds sit there in all that shivering, and shiver.

Easiest to call it weather—tree
with wind trouble, wren
with rain. But nature's nowhere without
weather, nowhere outside
ripples of relation, shifting, shimmering,
showering, still. The air

is parted, then departed:
seeming soaks
the fabric of it, the physical
fact, where I had always loved
the thought of God: without
material, he has no act.

*

The cars approach and then get swallowed up
in wet hedge, shine transmogrified to hiss;
the hedge grows fast and faster on this
diet of wet traffic, deepening my ear and eye.

The kids arrived by air from several
thousand miles away; they wore their Walkmen
even when they slept. They made a mental map
of airwaves: "You get KISS here!", said

the twelve-year-old. I said I fear
it's not the same. "You should have sent them

somewhere else," said the Bulgarian. "He isn't famous,"
I said kidward, "for his tact." "He's not

a lot of things," the eight-year-old replied,
"you should have thought of that

before you married him." I wanted then
to tell the children everything—the ins and outs,
the ups and downs, beginning with it wasn't
want of thought that got me married.

    *

What was it Angelus Silesius
was said to have remarked?
The eye I see God through
is the same eye
through which God sees me?

It shakes the ground of
human being. (Ultimately, what
is underlying us?) A stretch of ordinary

landscape can become
a luxury—the grains
of greens, the ripples off
a headland, ground as figure's

emanation . . .

    *

Women had been sent away so there would be no scenes
but when their friend had actually drunk the cup of poison
then the men broke down like women, and they wept.

    *

In time the saying
that-is-you-there-in-the-mirror
turned to this-is-me (for who can bear
the proper this-is-I? One is
embarassed, almost, putting oneself
in the nominative, there where it is not
entirely the objective's opposite . . .).
The mirror is the marriage,
or the language is.
We put ourselves in it.

It put ourselves in it. We put
itself in it. It put ourselves
in us.

*

Tell me what I'll have to do, he asked
the man who bore the cup. You drink it
and you walk around until your legs feel heavy,
then lie down. You'll feel the coldness

in your feet, and then your groin, and when it reaches
to your chest, it will be over. Only

wait, there's time, don't do it
yet, the friends began to beg. He answered

no, it's better I face up to this at once.

*

These floatings, flutterings,
these scraps of utter
delicacy,
petal-tissue,
white, with sunlight
in them, filled to the cells

with definition, all they are
is pairs of pure appearance:
little flappers in the grasses
of a summer. What comes over me
to see such butterflies, where no
bulldozing yet has drowned their soundings out

comes over me as something
monstrous: it's a tenderness,
the kind I felt abroad in nations,
seeing all the human variations on
a theme of vulnerability . . .

*

Can't you tell us something else? asked Crito.
But the cold had risen to the face
and frozen every answering away.

When Crito saw it, then he closed
his mouth and eyes.

And so "We owe a god an animal" became
the final words of Socrates.

32 Adults

(1990)

1

The world begins
with the apple of an eye (a figure
full of aperture that thinks itself
unseen, but is, in fact, rather a blind
headland of sex and saxifrage).

2

Half longing and half
sunstripe. Half sky and half
digested breast. Half whole.

3

Sporting the hat and cane of fancies, I
(a martinet at Easter) went up
without climbing. There are other
summers, other women, under one.

4

One draft of his wickered weather and
we wove mohicans with malls, ideogram
in intent, mind in bones, money in bars.
Sometimes simple
circumstance stands in.
Even a steel rod can be made to weep.

5

Outsmarted by every instance of reaper,
outwitted by every
ness of eliot and loch,
I hoarded blades,
held sway with old saws,
glued my gladioli back. I felt my way

toward lapidated specialty,
long-lasting frog and plug.

6

Queen of tricolore, I was born for ribbons,
born to make navies, not
waves (god too has a special
interest in the English
nation). The wrench and cross will be
my ornaments, our name

be done. Let all now close our eyes.

7

An invention raises
the food of my feeling from its mine
by powers of depersonalist contraption.
Rest at stomach, rest at heart! But ah, what
wooden wings groan it from sternum to
esophagus: the work of being is all

chug and track, deaf bluff. After,
I'll blunder on toward livings.

8

Isn't a pirate afraid? Isn't a sheep
adrift? Shake daggers, bandanas of fake
moustache and brandishes of bone—what's in his mind
but blotted-out ideals? The sky only

a sky, and the insect
likelier than his kind ever
to survive (for men are run through
with mentality: a long line piked
by EEG). And what

could save him, anyway,
who'd always looked
for animals in clouds, but found instead
a cloud in every lonely animal?

9

It hurts to have the skies grind
granite round my own
slow mortifying zones. God's name

is plain, but far too terrible to hear.
I'd like to make instead the best

of it—a yam souffle, or Jarlsberg yam—
I'd eat his words. But first must take

a scrub-brush to the stone.

10

Whirled for umpteen decades underwater, I
turned nebulae around—got inlets,
downlets, winklings caught

in all my turtled fronds; each garland took
a little finspin, till I felt
the petticoat updrawn
(that must be where

the man sank in).

11

Do the dead need a wet-nurse?
The flesh is a bandage where
being is wound.

12

First he put his
thumb into my eye,
and then he hung
the feathers on me.
That's O.K., I bide
my time. He likes
me gotten up. One day
I'll up and get.

13

My kind of beauty's monumental, so
they say. I can't see it (it's
in the eye, that most
transparent of progenitresses).
Still, a beam's a beam, and I'll
be built on, I'm a founding

figure, bearing up and up.
If History is ported
(com, re, pur), it can't hurt me.
I wasn't born, but made.

14

Did you catch those jack shades?
learn that turban? twist
that grin? Where did you get that
mercenary flair, my friend, how did you find
yourself in my mirrors? Must we agree?

15

After the blizzard of strictly
illicit kisses, sotto sofa, was rebuffed
he took a stern turn inward
(beak and beseeching
retracted for good, but one
eye rueful toward the old
bird dirt).

16

Ship-shape, abreast to windward, with my
feathers laid cross-wise and hatchwork calm
to all affront, I went out perfectly
bedecked. Where else
could I go? The world was ahead.

17

Fallen rhesus, laid in sharp caves
topped by standard wind-socks (good
was west) I toppled
onward, rocked into a kind
of evolution. Then
a thought had me: why gods and ghosts
were anyway invented. All's
a slant, and the pyramid sinks.

18

The pencil's point is my medulla:
I'm on automatic, shaving more and more

to make a face, and now and then emitting
small puffs of weather (that's my portrait
of imagination). Once I was soft armature,
becoming, you might say; but now I'm down
to vapor trail and fractured fusilage.

19

Invention of print, checks, chunks
of hygienic architecture (tile to take
fluid out), his shadow is cast
across cloud to reveal
the true interior (as god's
material): teeth and tickets,
jaw with lodgers, chockablock.
The junkhold of
our structure talks.

20

Left eye only, to be wound around
the overcomer: one is partial.
I'm all set: some smoke's in sight;
a whiff of cat, two legs of
Eiffel Tower or an avenue from air:
perspectives tend to fall into
last vestiges of looker.

21

Like a knot at the neck one's respectability
has its drawbacks. Two faces
(night and day) grow from the same gag,
and I'm capable of drool and cowlick,
upcrop, gas. A body catches
itself thinking, we should come
from the grove and build us one
brick moonrise. But colors keep trespassing
onto the scene from below, and tendrils enter into it,
undo the mental architecture. One field turns
into another: sliding greens
have found their middleman in me—
collared, panting back and forth
in alternating meanwhiles.

22

Rock took wing, or wave,
and the work of distinction's begun, one fin
to jigsaw the fabled cliff
between sky and earth or
animal and mineral or
here and now. What's cracked
from thunder and a puddle isn't wise:
it's mankind's angling lifeline. Thereafter,
however hard we try, we can't from falling
tell flying; prefer to live on the wind-worked strip
where one word breaks from two, without is weathered
into with, no platitude of progress can abide,
and separation woos
whatever has been monolith.

23

Do I put on airs, or is this
rather a bandaged skull, full of
cottage comforts, leaking little
brooks, brigades of the familiar
running in and out? Everything I won
I stuck stones on and flagged,
or hauled across the far toward the near, past
tremors of tree and wallets of swale, till all
was mine, though rivulets may tighten and the world

be bone unchaste.

24

I speak to you straight from the gorge,
the chasm where chastenings
come from, full (when everything else is brightest)
of the deepest dark. So utter am I
you begin to think in pairs, invent
some selves and echoes I'll have
none of. Listen here, nearer:
what you cannot see

are my eyes; my voice is what
(what with the plummeting)
you cannot hear.

25

At the heart of identity (which is
the universe) is nailed
a grid. For look-out or lock-up? All

the firing squad needs
I keep thinking
is a post and wall

and a hole to look through,
in death's instrument. Material
fills the mouth. Death's instrument's a head.

26

Mouse bones pile up by the cheese.
A cricket-world is seen under the arch of the cricket-leg,
the cricket to the cricket
crops up everywhere. Its joint
is smoking, jumping, a crèche

of wicks, a niche of crack. Tucked in a tendon's wish
are nine or ten of the acquitted. To themselves
it's everything, to us
a disappearing trick.

27

The scholar's head is swept toward
the scholar's specialty (in this case
the left glass, maybe monocular); it is swept from

the right hand, where the remains of a timekeeper
work at the temple. The scholar's always
contemplating some or other

bible; and he puts only two things
(all space, all time)
between him and the world.

28

My top hat got cocked oddly
on the problem of bones.
A shot went off my left side, lights
cast everywhere. We grew

these patterns underwater; sunk
is a dominion
of upside-down umbrella.

29

King Claus, the regal fool, has risen free
from his dreambed, where he felt
the sunrise light one eyebrow. Now he's full
of phrase and trapping, feeling himself
(from cheek to nose) to be real. At his heart
the barnyard fakes a ferocity, but is rather
attracted to downfall's
smoke and drape.

30

Goggle-eyed, broken-nosed, and bound
about the head (how high can a pate
be expressed?) he's most ill-set
about the mouth, which has
a gruesome grin or granite stuck
in it. Nomenclatures want

more than anything
there utterly to
possess him.

31

I am my own pedestal, I prop my whole
self up, with a side-burn of rubbing
and a comment off-put. I'm all

aside, long in the face of
some forecoming. Worry has rattled
the marbles in my eye-sockets, sent cracks

straight from my innermost fear
to the world's worst
faults.

32

Roped barely in the hold,
held hardly in the broken,

one feels outside as it were
a weight of unwept water. One must
not weep, one has almost become one's
medium, the boat by which
one's bound, bolted
and fastened forth . . .

Uncollected Poems

(1975–1986)

Postcard from Provincetown

It's not the provinces, exactly, though
four hundred miles away you are
the heart of civilization, to my mind.
At hand, my loneliness perceives

the waterside's cubes and blocks amounting
(four mere miles away, across
parabolas of bay, with late
sun crazing them) to gold. Extending

hurts, so I intend. My window's full
of shorelines gone; the gulls
slide by, symmetrical
in wind and glass. Anoint

my future, o amazing memory.
The only boat
is two boats, leashed
to a single puncture point.

Circus

What did I think I was bringing her into?
A wheel of easy colors,
beasts without a burden to their name?

The rage is for
exchange of meat. Poised on a pin of wits
the cat is belted into dance; the elephant on pain

of punishment, five times upon
the shovels of its toenails, kneels
for peanuts; soon the sky itself becomes

a close gray tent, and all the animals on earth
familiarized by narrative, belittled.
Knowing what we know,

how could we give a child
this stale balloon, balloon of breath?
Whichever way it goes

it goes some kind of wrong—
whether she loses it too soon,
or holds it too long.

Sebastian's Mirror

For clarity, for insight,
for star-fire, for fear,
for good, for given up, and for
the middle ground (beneath the flying mind)
she might

have spent all hours
at an open window. Near

at hand, behind her thirty
ideas of the world revealed,
the visible was struck, a bevilled
bargain with the planet Mercury.
(Countlessness is kept
without an eye on it.)
Dear

reader, other self,
how much
is lost when we
are busy dreaming? Being isn't

being DONE. And everything is one
die shaken: that's the secret
of the DNA. The iceways broke

in brilliant staves and bracelets,
and a whole God turned

into a partial girl, so wet she burned
her way into the dark. Behind her eyes,
behind her back what do

you see, as she admires the mirrors?
Everything so long
mistaken for oneself

is there: a breath of h's,
sleep of z's, the two that end
in eros . . .

A

A man of letters is of letters wary
though they grow and wane like any
other cloud; they make an amanita or a mandrill;
once we monikered a bomb and it

was partly Tour Eiffel (for cerebrating
miritary might) and partly
fungal outburst, viral
outburst, burst

of life (what are
we turning
to?). Remember, numbers
brought to grief

make greater grief, as surely as they make
great names; so named,
and wary, men go by

the acronym the instinct
underlies. The fingerprint
is shallow but it lasts.

The finger's deep as DNA, but dies.

Just Man

A little mud
they liquored up with lightning—
or a matter of
arithmetic—

four elements, two sexes,
thirty-nine books of begat?
From the ken of lust
come mull and dicker, some

unreasonable accommodation
(twig or straw or maybe,
in a blue moon, brick).
The Russian fable you incanted had

its magic, as a lullaby
(the orphan feeds the doll and then
the doll's not dead). Today you lie
and don't reply

beneath the sign of rock.

*

Maybe the cattle do not talk
because they are of undivided mind.
They wear rude rugs and never mope
about how much is missing. That's

OUR big idea, the world in two
possessive hemispheres—we keep
the animal routinely in the third
(and rarely in the second)

person. But his throes
are eloquent, who has no time;
the moment's endless, on his
urgent premises (stall, stable and flank

of a hill. The thinker's couch
seems narrow by comparison, expensively

upholstered in semesters—). Mates
may bite, a brother kick, but who'd

refuse the angel, just because the angel
bore a sword? Who'd pull the bush because it stood
to burn? Who'd say let's jail
the freedom-loving dove, because it might

just not come home? Just man.

Live

Coals work in a stove like
starter, yeast, some kind
of virus, actually
alive: the log

can catch it.

But we?
The typewriter has got
a case of nerves; the TV's
purpling its heroines. The girls

are wired and so abide
the boys; the slug trade
glistens, vacuum aspiration thrives.
Hired by the happy medium, we're free
to strike. Big trucks

with hoses come
to parking meters, sucking
them and septic tanks alike.

Five Threes (Fast Bike)

The baby stood to understand.
First forms, last words—
their adjectives have made them small.

There's not a box on earth
to hold the quick, a moon
to hold the man. But then

the ticketed parade begins—
the writing, recess, talking back
and band. The weeks

went by. To come
was chemistry. To go
was food. Meantime

they averaged out the pets,
numbered the fingertips and set
seven spokes by clockhand.

Two Holidays

1. Memorial Day

Don't smell, said the little girl.
The mother rolled her window up.
On my wrist the sweat
hit 98.7. (This was before
Celsius.) The little girl got out
mock make-up in compacts, panties for
days of the week. You keep this up,
her father said, you got a future. Wallets
and watches for all my little ladies! Where

do you get off, he turned to me. Just past
the fishwharf there, the bar (where I will kill
a bottle and what time I please,
shoot what pool I can,
what breeze . . .)

2. Christmas Eve

The TV's busy. No one
turned it on. Brad is amused
by the Brad-doll ad. A television once
went two point something years in some
bank window somewhere, so
the television says. It shows
a picture of a TV set, subtitled ACTUAL
REENACTMENT. Outside (if there IS

an outside) colored crèches
hum into the dark, a swarming sound,
investors, stock exchanges, change—it's all
in my head—America, fixed on skillets, quiz show questions,
high-priced spreads. On the couch a purple
textbook lies, PSYCHOLOGY it says, and harbors small
suspicions: men are attracted
to red, but women to blue. I'd say the virgin mothers need

some pain relief, with all those
animals around the house. Nobody turns

the television off. A ringing goes on
in the ears, and even deeper,

in the brain, a bright
department store where everyone on earth,
oblivious and busy, rushes after hours,
deepening the debt . . .

A Night in a World

I wouldn't have known if I didn't stay home
where the big dipper rises from, time
and again: one mountain ash.

And I wouldn't have thought without travelling out
how huge that dipper was,
how small that tree.

For a Sad God

I know God doesn't need my pity,
and Spinoza says pity's a low
emotion, still

it hurts my heart a little just to think
of God's having to be
so everywhere at once—

no lumping up
in addresses or throats, no
hankering or humoring allowed for Him, no big

investment in a Self, in anybody's
self, not a single
partiality like

what (erroneously, yes) we know
as love. And so I send
to God my humble

range of sympathies (how mean my mountains,
rivers, eye-rays
now appear). I

understand no all-or-nothing (although
human love has its own awful
all-or-nothing it can practise

failing at). I understand attachment and
its cutting, care and its
sad pseudonym. I know God doesn't

need my pity, but if God is man
I fear I fell—I mean
I feel—for him.

The Song Calls the Star Little

Something gets into us at night—
it's bigger than we dream or dare.
We lose our own domestic light,
we see too far.

But dawn arrives, and we
are pre-Copernican again;
the day revolves around
a rented skylight. Now to pay

for the apartment.

        *

Technically a day's required
to comprehend a day and night;
the logic of
the language weighs
much more than any
mind can bear. Don't think

of it, don't get
to thinking, no one has
that kind of time. Get up, forget

the double helix, shimmering
with worlds, your business is
this world, this day for your
forgetting. Make

a pot of the predictable,
a habit of the Times, get up, forget

the dream of
someone ill, and someone sad
and someone wandering in black—you're not

yourself! get up! set all
these moon-ideas and star-designs
aside, or you'll
end up (God help us)

really late at the lamp factory.

Faith

Electric lines are ripped from trees,
the blinds and bathtubs dangle,
chalk blooms high into the air
and dozers scrounge in the exposed
rubbish of interiors.

A letter's dated half a century ago
to someone in the penitentiary.
You got to have a faith unshakeable, she wrote.

And now from morning until dusk
the workers rip and roar, they
pound and they resound until
translucent air becomes a thick
acoustic medium, breathable air a test of dust,
and one whole streetful of amazing residences,
intricate with human life, inscribed
with human history, becomes

a vacant lot. This is the nothing
someone so emphatically wanted.
I stood for hours at a nearby window
and could see a hundred years undone;

but there remains untouched a space they never made,
the kind of space they could not fill.
There is a sky they cannot deconstruct,
a clarity that moves to its own tune.
We may not hear, the sun is deafening, our lives
a din of disregards, but don't let worldly
meanings shake your faith:
there IS a moon.

Kind of Poor

The cemetery suburb was
a plastic Florida, with permanent
bygones, slow
begonias, partial
birds of paradise. Always was
our happy hour—where we could ever
after live. We wrote more o's and x's
on our checks than anywhere; the i's and u's
let a hug come between them. Now and then we happened on

a funnybone box, and in the throat
a built-in rattle, dimly evidentiary.
(Maybe nothing would end the line
which we had reckoned
vector; maybe nothing ended after all
with molecules and atoms, anything a word
holds still.) Gestations

in crystal, charm
in finch and quark! Despite
our hesitations, shoots put out
a billion pollinating stars.
Great human wealth

was concentrated in a child,
who with one blade of grass could whistle up
immunity against enormity.

For a Good Man

*Though the spirit needs time, an instant
of it is enough.* —W. H. Auden

Any little mirror holds
the sun's entire
untouchability.

A drop of water carries
countless populations:
seconds split

into a fan of decades,
singlenesses into
daughters. Any memory

is made of dream, and any dream
of dynamite: a candled bar
and grill can drink

the drinker out of sight.
I felt, I really
felt you; then

the multitudes were numbing.
Any knifewound now is every
one I had coming.

Lifelike

The news gave me a scare. I tried to look
innocent, tried to look
elsewhere. But all the world

is in the living room, there is
no other place, and five
fast channels of tornado went on

devastating Xenia,
the surgeon's family went on being
murdered by the surgeon, urban areas would soon be linked

by bullet train, with mail deliverable even after
nuclear attack. I'm
scared. I think

my pilot light is out.
Perhaps these warplanes (audible
and visible) are real—a real

old building falls. Is this
the weather or a window? Where are you?
(Can anyone be true at all

so far away?) I turn
the TV off but then I see
the box with me inside it, small and gray.

Disappearee's Song

My father fell asleep in his new life.
Trees are being made
deciduous in my earshot by
incessant shimmering. Someone is shaking
paperclips in jars. The wavework is

immediate and deep, and full of particles
of lives (the children, houses, offices and years)—
talk's yellow tatters, reason's seed
float every sure identity away.
Had I been had

by someone in a dream
or by myself, a spirit whose preoccupation with the body
led to occupation? An indrawn breath
thickens into shape; the body spins
some threads, with fists and fibulas,
and something comes of nothing, comes

to bloom in a crown of creed,
in a splash of flesh. And then
the breath goes out. The pool
gets clear; in waves and particles
a point is missed,
a partner disappears.

The Act

The drunk crowd hoots the fat emcee.
He drops his face, he checks his fly,
he waves the singer forward. She
has scars to show
how someone sometime
missed her eyes.
The catcalls multiply;
all she can do is sing.

And sing she does, and all
falls still. Her song is sweet enough
to raise us from ourselves—and you who never
were promoted and he who harbors
bitterness from cancer

float away; the lovers lose their senses of
a world to be against; the ironists
are made to drift in rivulets of petal . . .

Out of doors, it's zero. Stars
are everywhere. Two thousand miles
across the frozen lawns, the emcee's mother
leans beneath a kitchen light. She does what she has done
each other Friday night: she polishes the emcee's
little shoes—the brilliant ones, of bronze.

Where

I leave the drink and cigarette
where the music is, and go

outdoors where nothing
is the whole idea.

The winter zeros in on eyes and
orphans everyone, and clear

is not a kind of thought.
Outside you're not

as gone as in a house.
How differently we saw

the painting called "The Empty Chair."
It showed two chairs, identical except

one held a hat. (Which *is*
the empty chair, I asked; you thought

the question trivial. I thought the hat
an extra emptiness.) Between

"a room" and "room" you didn't
mark the article of difference. A knife

fell on the bed, the ruler we had
on hand. I must have missed you when I was

the one that I was thinking of. I came inside again and left
the feeling in the glove.

Household

Everything goes
into the stove, a kind of detox where
the diaper is purified, the kotex smokes,
the orange peels go spicy and the black wood gets
a red-hot buzz. Give me a hand, the bluer woman said;
they threw the book at her; some red rubbed off.
All help will end up

deepening the taboo puddle. We,
ablaze or icy, are our best
dilemma. Every day the coronary fabric
wears a little thinner, trouble being
habit, truth a dream. O man, my

flesh and blood, my only
kind in the furnace of
natural cruelty, help
to sort the never from the known. If living's
something made, a property we're on,

who might attach it? Are we stuck
in stuff? Help bury all these bones, or else
let's build a whole new homestead, out of hatchets.

To a Christian

Episcopal, that church I visited at first
was awfully goddamn subtle, let me tell you,
all its miracles resigned to metaphor, its marvels made
off-white (on which the best suspended X
was intellectual, its wire imaginary and its matter gray;
it didn't have a serif to its name, and no

man dying, either). I was more
attracted, therefore, to
the Catholic church, that good
stiff wallop of the bodily when you walk in,
a cool sepulchral stone, cold sweat. At least there seemed
some substance to the ideogram, some body to the love.
Red mud and wrap of wind, weren't we
what happened after Mars and Venus mated?

All the alcoves harbored
statuary saints. In one, a well-fed mother
held a baby God, above a big blue world.
She sat there on a solid cloud, not quite
alone—*mirabile dictu*, a dog
of similar proportions there beyond the world
was carrying a torch at the tip of her foot, a foot
from North America. I put

a candle on the North Pole, which was up.
I lit one in Saint Rose's alcove, too, because
you loved the zone of roses, loved
the swollen feeling, risen reds,
a kind of carnal fever that
undid you, rotting what
was rich. You loved

in point of fact two men:
one offered cool eternal life, the other
death, but with a kiss. So help me God,
as I'm alive, I can't tell which is which.

A Hurricane Can Cast

its storming color-load
(wavelengths of gleam and bruise)
to trouble us full days before
wet actuality, and whipping scene.
My father and his father told of this,

time after time. But I was slow;
I couldn't see the stars already
racing off to leave us here,
in wakes of pinkened shift.
It's fifty years before a person

seems to get the drift: the storm in us is nothing
next to the storm we're in; and the storm we're in
is plainer yet: it's simply nothing next.

So there we have it. Every generation,
brand new disbelief. And through it all the thread
of someone crying, someone trying
to escape—we've got a mind
to turn the channel, fool the funnel, sing
a song about The Truth. The eye, after all,

is raised. From space it looks

so peaceful, so aloof—a meteorologist's
mandala! But heavens aren't
where people live. They live
down here. And down here

people drown on roofs.

Denomination

The radio fades. The blues are out, and then
the stars. By dark we mean
well, full of firewater.

We have saved the old songs,
solid gold, and to
what end? The houses pass
as in a movie from
a hundred years ago (inside, in summer,
thieves can lift
whole windows of yellow). The car comes

to a full stop. The graveyard's made out
in bare moon: here we are,
stock-still, at the end of the line.
Some words are lost

for being far, and being far
too often said. What's in
a name? It's time, they never
told you that. So lovers come
to visit cemeteries. There you don't need any

date to understand
how long a Hope or Patience has been dead.

Literal

All those flourishes and curlicues were his
best irrepressibility—each letter
traced in the air with a toetip, each fine
detail of trill in the gardened uprush.
Hollows needed him
in order to resound—there he began
to spin his hammock out
of palm and text and unspent sex.

And then he got so sick
he couldn't get from bed.
The sheet was signed with shit and he himself
at thirty-seven, stricken by that fact,
was hexed by people's kisses, vexed by people's energies,
the very wrath of ornament turned on
itself, its former favorite.

Finally he dropped the chromosome bible,
cared no more for calligraphic nature,
x's of treasure or animal track.
Death moved him, far
from laughter, far from figured lights and darks and far
from foreign and familiar time. I left his house
and walked among the monuments, in parks.

And that was when I saw the ferns—
arising everywhere from warmish ground,
promiscuously pale, preeminently question-marks.

Poems from Dangers

(1968–1977)

Spectacles

I don't move
but the grass in the window
does an utter
smear campaign. The trees revert

to wet green, and the irises
with a saliva of high shine
cast even the mud of what I can see
blue as a colorfast blood. I'm no longer

a man of distinction: a window fills
with resemblances, a face like mine, an evening's
long damp beard like lawn. The paperboy appears
to wheel familiarly across my vision, trick

of doubles, only to leave
warped tracks. This is no news,
good news. I don't move
in the dark. My wire-rimmed glasses

sprawl on the desk, either a bright
suggestion to the uncorrected
eye, or a small
wrecked bicycle.

Orbit

The woman with one glass eye
will cast no stones, will name no sinners
in the sleight-of-hand show; knows
the house is in her head.

The eye's not quite
opaque; the world
is breakable. She buys it anyway—
its shaking bed, its line of sweets and
scenes that do their own dissolves.

Tonight the moon is two

quarters, into which
she moves, reflective.
Seeming has a zero at
its heart, and sum and
difference have put
their arms about
the woman with one glass eye.
She's half asleep, half keeping

watch, her dreams a dim
swerve and a longing and a wide
lens into which
distortion lets

a man's face sink or swim.

Pupil

A little person, I lean in your eye.
A language already translated, I rise
when you call on me. I ride the sea
of your person like troubled sheep,
become another in your

image: every one is
two-faced. This is living, in
arithmetic or sin. Declining, I'm
as single as the moon that sinks, the moon
that climbs the walls. We keep refining grammars, keep
our senses. Certain bodies make for certain
tides. A little lean, I eat in your eye.

It takes a seer to know one. Men
circle the earth, they eat from east
to west. Nothing pronounces them
alone, not even sleep
goes unconjugated. Only I, inclining
like the sun, reverberate. A lot

of you, I lap and graze on your rocks.
A little me, I learn in your person.
When you point your finger, my mouth doubletalks.

Preferences

Antarctica is no place for the eye
that loves a mesh of interlacing, knot
of growth. The plain truth oversimplifies
the human state. The southern senses set
a trap of fictions: stick and wire to stir
up single-minded nature, complicate
the unanimities of cool with fur
and fine desires. The draftsman tolerates
no unassuming page, but goes about
unearthing all its bones; the ink insists
on fibulas and femurs, none without
the knob of trouble's ends, the double kiss
that terminates the clean sweep of the shaft.
The belly of a hill has got a fault
of birth corkscrewing inside out; the craft
of architects can make a skulling vault
out of a fever of ideas or tilework of
details, and listeners warm to the song
when wildnesses are made to cool, to scale.
The heart's two-timing, thicketed and wrong
but reason doesn't simply make us single.
In the woodland latitudes we grow
to love the shrub's uplifted etch and tangle
over the amnesias of snow.

In Praise of Pain

A brilliance takes up residence in flaws—
a brilliance all the unchipped faces of design
refuse. The wine collects its starlets
at a lip's fault, sunlight where the nicked
glass angles, and affection where the eye
is least correctable, where arrows of
unquivered light are lodged, where someone
else's eyes have come to be concerned.

For beauty's sake, assault and drive and burn
the devil from the simply perfect sun.
Demand a birthmark on the skin of love,
a tremble in the touch, in come a cry,
and let the silverware of nights be flecked,
the moon pocked to distribute more or less
indwelling alloys of its dim and shine
by nip and tuck, by chance's dance of laws.

The brightness drawn and quartered on a sheet,
the moment cracked upon a bed, will last
as if you soldered them with moon and flux.
And break the bottle of the eye to see
what lights are spun of accident and glass.

The Score

One puts on one's white socks,
one by one, expecting the geraniums
to stay put in the storm, stay red
in black weather, saying nothing.
One puts on one's white shoes,
hearing the far uninterrupted
alarms of children as one ties them,
puts one's feet together, opens the door
and passes the plants one favored once
and potted, five by five. One knows

one's places, seconds the sea's slant
on things, wants the love one believes
is native to harm. Accountably reaching

the cliff, one will unaccountably
dive. Upon reflection,
one will be two,
racing into each other's arms.

Ozone

These trees have the many circles of self-love.
Their leaves ring and ring, and the fingers
are fat, and arms have a grab on the trunk, grove
in its own groove, as moving as trees can get.

And what I cannot get around
(in which upside-down trees are hung)
is the cipher, the fact, of this pond.
It hugs and doubles what is upright and downgrowing,

which we may be said to be, and trees must.
Under rainfire, my face in the water splits: above
and within the transcription of my own cast
lines, I, I have the many circles . . .

To See the Light

It is nothing till it takes
residence in things: in the window, with
its rope of ivy, it turns all the little
envies face by face
transparent, infiltrates and etches,
makes the network float. Inside the room
the vessels fill with light and rise
as weightless as suspicion: tissues
on a shrink's glass tabletop.
But once inside, it suffers
a change of nature—fixtures
of imagination, filaments of affection,
human ways of lighting up. A man is waiting

close, to analyze my cries. He snaps a switch,
a tree of juice, a burning tree (if only we
could see through walls). I watch what happens
to the window's whip of living shine: as stung
as stunning, leaves hang on:
lit now by room, they seem more ap-
than trans-, as parents go. If they
can take it, I will try. The whole room
trembles, but I offer, lash
by lash, my naked eye.

A Few Licks

Because I am lucky, I'm a glutton
for sea punishment this summer:
for the discipline of the current
  backlash, bondage

of the temporary. Underwater
every air is heavy, every somersault
a motion slowed. The sun's
  a warp, aware

as any sidewise eye with fins.
I sink past reckon's isle and past
the lace of debt and shell of
  work, wreck

of pleasures. Under pressure
I cannot tell green from blacking
out, or greed from sacrifice, from
  kisser killer,

sense from sense. The vessels lie
inside and out, belying
interface. The eye directly
  feels, filled

with how it looks. I dive
to prove this place, to know
how deep in my luck is the loving
  hook.

Tendencies

A body is seduced by damages.
Swamp of bad blood, pump of glue,
it wants to wear a dress of bandages
and lose the human
teeth and hair it grew.
Led on a leash to the penthouse rail it feels
attracted to the forty-storey fall.
It catches in the wish
itself. Or then, unhaltered
in the flesh's patch of
all thumbs, it will choke on
mushrooms, soak its bones—
before it thinks to be sucked dry.
The man goes daily nose-down in the dead-
man's-triangle, to fill the purses of
his lungs with dirt. The normal child
will hold her breath (her own), will hear the sky
approach, and lurch from what she learned, and head
for what she'd otherwise forget.
Defiled, the body stumbles back for more;
unloved, it looks for luck. It comes when it
is called obedient. A woman, near the thin
ice of a man's regard, will start
(appalled and partial) leaning in.

Gig at Big Al's

There's a special privacy on stage.
Wearing little, then less, then
nudity's two silver
high-heeled shoes, I have

to dance, and I dance to
myself: the men are posed at tables just below,
importantly equipped with gazes of assessors
and the paycheck's sure
prerogatives—but they are dreams

I've realized, they are the made-up eyes. No one
knows anyone. I pull down dark around the room.
I turn on sex's juke two-step. I set
foot on the spotlight's

isolated space and grease
a hip and lick a leg. With a whip-
lash of gin in the first row, with
a beer can of bucks in the last, anybody can buy
my solitude (this multiple
circumlocution of crotch). But nobody

can touch me; by the law of California,
I can't "touch myself." So though it's all
complicit, none of it is public—not until

     in one side door
         on his soft shoes
              my lover comes to watch.

The Most

The dining room is empty at the country inn.
We are, for your comfort, far from the town
of your friends, of mates and mistresses, and of
amends. The maitre d', whose only prey
we are, brings pickles, beans in vinegar
and switches on the musical not even he
(left to his own devices) would have listened to.
My face is in the cup of my hands.
You consider it.

Around us a promiscuity of settings,
vainness of display—like mockeries of our
intentions, linens stretch untouched and white
as far as I can see. The fish will be

untender when it comes, but I won't have
the heart to say so; we will find ourselves
in other rooms, you wondering repeatedly
how long my husband works. For now we make

the most of our opposing faces. Waiters
come and go, you settle on a suitable
entree, the room grows huge, the afternoon
appears, a glaring error, waste
of windows. "What I hate,"
you say, "is public places."
I look around and see
uninterrupted emptiness.
The wine glass fills with sun,
a slow bright bomb. The mob in me sits still.

Outcry

She rides the last few minutes
hard, pressing her heels
in the stirrups, keeping what she can
concealed, a stone mid-fist.

But now she's grown too big, the room
too lit with wet. A man
has got a hand in her again, he wants
to pick her pocket, leave her flat.
The room begins to heave,
the white elastic walls of senses
wow, the words well up, the skin
must give and give until the sheet-

rock splits, the syllable comes
leaking from her lips:
her body breaks

in two. Spectators
grin. The sex
is speakable.
The secret's out.

Fable

The women are the makers of the men,
by hook and crook, by shuttle and by wool
of lifelong gathering. A dream supplies
a month of bundled sheep; a kitchen's fat
with fibs; the goat's to get. Long after dark
the men are raveled at a reddened stone
that beats back what cannot be seen, in kin-
dled twos, duplicity, the tongues of love,
the glossolalia of fire. The shoes
the men left empty after five will fill
with oranges of warm and talk of loose.
The women work their weaving into sleep,
the men are knit into the drowsy lie
that do is done and overly is deep.

And not until the tree of sons is lit,
and soup is turning brown upon the spoon,
and not until the yellow yarns are blue
and oil is risen reservoir to lip,
when art is burned on all their surfaces,
will women find their calling in a moan.
And not until the noun has known the verb
(in grammars learned by heart and not by rules)
to slip particulars and fit, will gown
be nakedness, and silver overall. And not
until they've spun nine spools of moon
may women lay their looming bodies down.

Patronage

The gate posts where the drive begins
are foursquare stands of
stones nobody cut: the masons found
their fit and native juttings,
bite of related teeth, yin and yang in rock.
They set them there to set, some hundred years,
some limits for an unencumbered life. I walk

from the lower lawn toward shelter, and the house
secures the very sense it flatters, batting its
shaded eyes, sprawling in awnings of parlance.
I'll eat my words for this, be what I eat,
say what I see: the open door

unrolls a red tongue at my feet.

Double Agent

I pledge allegiance to the old
country, the hourless
state, powers
of sleep.

I was born to sleep, given to love
its populations, floodgates, déjà vu,
its tunnels. I crave the escape
artistries of slaves, the neural
pathway and the shutter-quick
synapse. The mind is wicked, very well,

the judge is dead, the legislators
naked. And the plain girl has her
hairlips kissed
by the rubber sticks
of pilgrims. Her legs spread
rumors of deafmute victory, her fingers
and toes written with scripts
no one can reproduce. No one

keeps time, the watches stop,
and monasteries softly swallow men.
My citizenship is clear
as unpolluted airways, clear
as a carnivore's eye.
The girl gets

the queen's emissary
wet, who comes bearing
bacon, a message for me, who read meat.
The only remote possibility, a bruise at the skyline,
a fog at the edge of the world, is her
desire: the past she wants
is west, toward which

a moon or mood or metronome impels me.
And only then, in some extremity,
as the ship of the queen

or state is sunk or wrecked
on a radio wave do my
own eyes open
to the dimmest
human spectacles,
my ears fill up with harsh
and kitchen insurrections, cash
of electric light. The flag I am wrapped in
whitens into sheets. Surrender

is arranged. I am at home. I am in time.
Another fifteen minutes and I could have had
world history rewritten (through the long
omitted nights). I rise

to the occasion of the bathroom sink, and foam
at the mouth, naturalized.

Politics

The dog pauses before the fire,
watches, gains
weight, can't make
light of it, lies
heavy down. The geese immediately

freeze to the lake. The snake
wears a bad new wrinkle:
bark. And trees lie,
rattling skins;
and squirrels fib,
the purses of their faces full.
The fire spits up its splinter groups

of dimes, of flint. The arsonist
is lying, here and there; the bear
begins to snore, and every
outdoor animal expires
a rich white lie of air.
Even you
are taken in.

It is not winter.

Fix

I.

I needle April into letting go:
out of a white all winter
we mistook for poverty, the world turns
suddenly indulgent, dealing

pinwheels and color wheels, springing
songbirds down buttered wires, waxing
the lips of women red, unrumpling all
the hearth-devoted dogs. The senses

split their pods—switchblades hatch
in the hands of the *nouveaux riches.*
The eye gets flashy with a superficial wit
and jets flock to the big blue bedroom,

trailing their ribbons of emission.
Green has made its inroads in your eyes:
you envy all of nature. But I unzip
your outerskin, and basketsful of pink

and white carnations flower forth. My hands
are full of health, they tremble on the verge of your
having, the one hooked eye to go, one undone rainbow,
prism of liquid, lip of spill—

II.

Far and away the strictest sun
is stationed overhead, its lashes
keep an eye on us. We don't look up
from loving. Therefore he,

hell-bent on pleasure, readies
himself to come. He straps the fashionable

parachute upon his borrowed frame, and hums
a human tune. We hear him approach and then

we hear him hover there, for what seems hours,
in the season's wings, the near
obscene old god, revving and revving his
devil-may-care machine.

Excerpt from an Argument with Enthusiasts, Concerning Inspiration

I agree that something
greatens us,
but intelligence doesn't enter into it.
At the moment I can calmly say
that we turn certain
switches, certain
lights go on; that there are rational
tricks to make
things go away and things arrive.

But with whatever brilliance in
the middle of the night
in whatever living-room we sit down and discuss
what dead men know, things
we can only intuit
breathe in the room. The curtain
fattens and collapses, swells again. Nobody
hears his own voice right.

The mind is flashy, yes, but take
the stupid wind away and say what's left alive.

Breathless is dead, however bright.

Reservation

Let me never weigh the handiwork
of amorousness. Loving, gemini,
has for its lick and lash a fork
of tongues, for apple and for ache an eye.

I never want to know of your
endearment the dimension; on that cross-
hatched night our sense of care
turns paler, let's not calculate the loss.

Because the voice has moored a pair
of boats in every skull's marina; and because the teeth
will raise no single issue on the lip, because our kids will bear
us, upside down, in time, in their two-timing eyes, and not
    the least

because on every hand the body packs
its double-barreled heat, don't number
passions, do not ask
the caliber of loving, lest it name

a bullet after you. The measure
of your influence is feeling, countlessly again,
the senses fill the holes where pleasure
goes to father pain.

Against a Dark Field

Hate makes my head light.
Hate rides its particulars, styled
after fireflies, after envy. Our bed rises
on its liquid, I hate the heavy

body known, by rights,
as mine. The window's colony of wild
ideas, appointed, hovers. Wise
is lightweight. Undercover

I withdraw from us and turn
into pure fuel. You blacken with sleep. I green with burn.

Debtor's Prison Road

I.

They let me go
at night, minus my timepiece, lighter,
personal effects. The air is always shaking
the same jars of safety pins: cicadas.
Song is my recidivism: always
I'm abandoning the road to stand
(unwatched, unseconded) in someone's
field. The stars (that are not mine)

tick fitfully, they always have
appointments. Punctual, six-sharp,
they are David's; they have lodged in his
death tent, have stuck in his mud sleep. Bad luck

leaves me a loan: no company, no katy-
did or promissory
note or night
can last.
The air
loses its nerve,
the old saw its eyeteeth and I
my words—my alwaysing and my.

II.

In hush the repossessors reach
the edges of the field. They pass

for shadows, sheep of ambush, animals of
permanence. They turn a black beyond returning

and they haunt the sleepless. I don't count,
who cannot earn my keep.

It is 70 degrees in late November.
Opening a window, you nearly know

how certain
days filter themselves through
screen, chain
saw, sun
dust,

games of chance. How certain as cliché
certain days are. You make
a bed. Sunlight
runs in. The bed
reconciles everything. You know

how the far-off can surround you, how things swim
here, thousands of miles inland, of their own
accord, to find the unknown
passage of your
human ear.
You know now how

the times at times
can lose their most acerbic
edge, and your planned child
and your grandmother rise
as a sound and single sweetness in
the aural shell you carry
from amphibian history,
into the present, the shore
of rising, sinking
treasure. Just
don't blow it! History's

not pleasure, merely; even now
its sharks sharpen the future.
You nearly know it.

Stroke

The literate are ill-prepared for this
snap in the line of life:
the day turns a trick
of twisted tongues and is
untiable, the month by no mere root
moon-ridden, and the yearly eloquences yielding more
than summer's part of speech times four. We better learn

the buried meaning in the grave: here
all we see of its alphabet is tracks
of predators, all we know of its tense
the slow seconds and quick centuries
of sex. Unletter the past and then
the future comes to terms. One late fall day
I stumbled from the study and I found
the easy symbols of the living room revised:

my shocked senses flocked to the window's reference
where now all backyard attitudes were deep
in memory: the landscapes I had known too well—
the picnic table and the hoe, the tricycle, the stubborn
shrub—the homegrown syllables
of shapely living—all

lay sanded and camelled by foreign snow . . .

Solitary's Solace in the Natural Sciences

Axed at the
right point

wood snaps into strips
along its grain. Rocks too

crack, along pre-extant
tracks. Weakest at the spine,
down lines of symmetry,
the shell, the skull

tapped by a gentle hammer, tell
the halves (of life
beginning, and
life lost). We are most

vulnerable
where last
we were conjoined.
I hold this fact

in my fist
like a fifty-dollar bill,
like a future, like a first
unbreakable egg . . .

Poems from A World of Difference
(1977–1981)

The Field

It was my day to study
in the field. I found
fences strung with glass beads,
small possessions of shock (signs of his
and hers). I couldn't make myself
at home. I lowed,
so the cow would,
but the cow looked up,
misquoted. When I got back to the house
my five hired fellow-specialists

were taping their abstracts
to the window. Soon it would be dark.

The House

In evening purples, the kings
draw farther and farther away,

as absolute and cool as stars.
Dark brings its sexual powers to bear

until the trees outside are huge.
Help, I tell the deaf man. (Look,

I signal, to the man with broken eyes.)
The moon is in its seventh month. A truck goes by

with singing in its wake, an outside
chance. I've got to leave this house

where my uncle who has lost his hands,
my father who has lost his tongue,

decide that everything is relative.
They cannot mean the world to me,

turning to themselves,
taking the window for bad art.

Like

Always I have to resist
the language I have
to love. This is my work,

as the girl reflected
in the cowpond studies
frequencies of throb.

The meaning isn't deep.
I don't say yes to please.
Polite, the politicians

drop their hat of names
but I forget the first
and family of them, my life

will not stay memorized. Always
the days will be
longing for summer,

always the animals
falling in love—but always is always
like never before.

The Fall

Gold leaf fell
to the rake and the fire.
Leaping headlong into those
upholstered yards, we couldn't tell

rags from riches, loving a little
trash by nature, having
an orange crush. But love
becomes a set of pet

names, all diminutive,
and as for God,
we saw it was the dark
that made the stars. As time

went by,
the jeweled movement
of the loan shark's car
would utterly impoverish the sky.

At a Loss

Five quid for the sloth,
constructed of wickedness.
This is a value, says
the ultimate auctioneer.
Ten for a fence to sit on.
How much for
the sister of charity there?
the synaesthesiac with the loud shirt?

A child in the crowd keeps asking who it is
that makes the icebox light go on.
In some back room a counterfeiter
mans his press. He's making money
toward his own pet senator and pair
of reproducing angels.

Now the wisdom-tree is being sold
as firewood, felled
by lightning, overharvesting or just
an ax. The stroke may have cost us
our lives. Where

is the *genius loci* we were told
to look for? The father
says there is a little man
in each refrigerator, making
light of cold.

Mind

A man looks at his watch to see
if he's hungry. Yes, it's eight,
he's free to contemplate the whitefish,
white pepper, crème de la crème,
what his wife has made.
He says, You shouldn't have.
She says, Don't mention it.
The son grows thin.

At dinner the child tells a story,
what he saw outside: red hair,
a burning tree, a word on a sidewalk.
Mind your language, someone says.
He bites his tongue. At school

his days are numbered. He makes a felt
calendar, but that's not really
the idea. He has a hard time
understanding: color is
the frequency, and not the object.
They keep asking, Now do you see?

Soon he'll be old enough
to take Criticism, practise saying
So-and-So sounds deaf, So-and-So
looks blind. Outside, the firetrucks

leave the scene, a safe gray street.

Meantime

In the days when everyone said
oh boy and gee, when women were stoled
and muffed, and men would be men,
the hurricane her
seventh birthday was

her first idea of sex—
an undomesticated power no one could
withstand, whose outskirts would
bedraggle trees. She suffered
an infatuation. Many ladies later,

she'd recall the proper name for this,
but in the meantime, something had to be
made of boys, who kept
cropping up. Windmill of
ankles and wrists, she had to turn

thirteen.

Blue Streak

During the twentieth century chance
was the form we adored—you had to
generate it by machine. Kisses came

in twisted foil, we quickened the clock
with digitalis, invented the pacemaker, in case
we fell in love. The whiz kids were

our only ancestors: the buzz saw,
working west, had made its mark.
My children, this is history:

we made it! Millions counted!
One-of-a-kind was a lie! And the poets,
who should have spoken for us, were busy

panning landscape, gunning
their electrics, going
I-I-I-I-I.

Meaning Business

Gizmos and jeremiads aside, God
romped in a fit of glee, apropos
of nothing. He had no friends
in higher places—had no bailiwick
at all; he hadn't an inkling, a sou.

The writers, meaning business,
came calling him names.
They wanted him to say the word
was first and last—they wanted to live
for good. But God was a fool for his own

new feet, and a few
odd monosyllables of song. As long
as he lived, they'd have to
be content. Later, they could read
themselves into his will.

Confessionist

Busted and booked, and all
for love. We used to rip off
clothes, and lie, steal time alone.
I was taken with him.

Let me tell you it's embarrassing,
here in the haircut's architecture,
here in the secret chair.
I dwell on two antiques:
the moon, and the man that was in it
for me. We used to love the moving

amplitudes of radio—the earplug,
roadmap, fact faced in a blue clock.
Soon we'll have the afterlife
to love. And in the meantime

artists take to the networks,
cackling doppelgangers as their stunt-men.
All you have to do is wive
your innuendi, bring the whole house down.
Trash is material, truck of hunches,
fridges and ovens of dump.

After the frontal lobotomy
you know no one from two
in the echo chamber,
no one from Adam.

Impressionist

1

I wasn't getting anywhere.
What good was the book
of matches, watch
of wheels, defective
mechanisms of my sex?
Where was the most of myself
I meant to make? Mistress

of the minded Q, the pointed I,
I knew discretion comes to order
and the million likenesses add up
to one distinction (cells of
color, on a riverbank,

where the French
girl in the light
blue dress remembers
someone gone).

2

My mechanic lights a cigarette.
I'm at his desk, revising
the bill. I take a zero out,
I move a dot: this makes all

the difference. He wants
to sell me speed: I need it
like a hole in the head (my head
is overweight). I mean the world

to him. He'll fix my Comet,
I will feed his Milky Way machine.
I mean it matters, mud or moon,
what grounds we have for understanding.

Now I'm getting somewhere,
driving it home. The roadside leaves

are orange, yellow, every kind
of down. A dust of light

is in the drawing room, a dust of flowers
in the living room, and in the bedroom, dust
has almost filled
the eyecup of the dead impressionist.

Whoosh

What summer hasn't shaken
its share of flourishing
girls from arbors where,
aloof, they could

forbear? What summer hasn't
brandished its swatches
of daffodil *accompli?* It makes
a memorable decor, that

twisted Mississippi, with its five
willows for whoosh. The girl you courted,
pendant from a swing, is there forever
in her weightlessness of veils

while the woman you married
once and for all walks out
(in fall, in tight
black pants) and bears

a heavy heart into the avenue.

Stall

Through memory and actual
mud, the woman approaches

a deep red barn where animals stand
for anything—for years, for food, for good.

The woman is looking forward
to the day when everything is clear. She thinks

she's due for sunlight, freedom from
all kinds of kin, but then

a moan from a downwind stall reminds her
of the man who had

his way with the dark in her.

Hag

*a kind of light said to appear
at night on horses' manes and
men's hair—Oxford English Dictionary*

Horse gets into me, its mane
electric and its hooves

drumming up business. Men
get into me, having the hair

to go outdoors. I call
for order, but the cop's a cut

below; my songs grow
fur and hide. Horse

shoots up the spine, the arms
of stars, stopping what moves

in its tracks. Combed for romance, the moon
will disregard its caretakers. The groom

stands up in bed, ready to bridle at
a moment's notice. All the night,

the fences down, the animals steal
from a newlywed's side, to wander

where a woman cannot come, who kept
her word but gave away her light.

High Jinx

Either they treed me, or I hid
in the weed, or wash
was my overcoat, or drink
was my wish. Either they missed

my face in the tea, or my stink
in the hash, or my hand
in the honeysuckle. I've been wanted
seven years, and wasted more; been

burned, interred. Either they didn't
fertilize me, or I turned
to a desert rat; either I jumped ship
or they dumped me; I was game

or they shot my pool
with lily-killer. Man. Either you
used up your stunt juice or
my antibody grew.

North Island Songs

The water that made the island
murdered the men. You can't expect
these moons to last, these fallen
roses, rising gold. You can't believe
in pure decor or easy virtue.
People are dying for good.

    *

He wants other women,
those who never leave
well enough alone.
He's well enough.

At a distance I gather
what is going on. The dark
that fills the deep is the song
they hear in hulls.

    *

If I pine and croon I am no woman
in my hooked heart, if I stand for lying,
maybe I can take a shine and still
keep cool. In its own element

that tough old bird the gull
hauls across the last-chance bars
and flashy waterfront its evening
seine of wail.

    *

The dance turns out to be
a woodfire, fellows from the factory and mill,
a cop in the doorway looking nowhere,
and a kid to stamp our hands. The band
is bored by the third song and the man I'd like
to like is drunk in a swarming corner, so
I plunge out the storm door toward the cars and there

are stars, all out. Orion perfectly
speared by a pine. The moon exactly
sharpened by a shade
of meaning.
I can think now

cold and clear, imagine
why the inland people call
some kinds of water kill.

Language Lesson 1976

When Americans say a man
takes liberties, they mean

he's gone too far. In Philadelphia today I saw
a kid on a leash look mom-ward

and announce his fondest wish: one
bicentennial burger, hold

the relish. Hold is forget,
in American.

On the courts of Philadelphia
the rich prepare

to serve, to fault. The language is a game as well,
in which love can mean nothing,

doubletalk mean lie. I'm saying
doubletalk with me. I'm saying

go so far the customs are untold.
Make nothing without words,

and let me be
the one you never hold.

Toward an Understanding

1. On High

Up here I love light, travel
light. Sun runs its slick
liquids down each arm
and wrist and fingerlake
on earth. Pack-rat of scrap shine,
I catch the filaments of foil
that twist through green-brown tweed,
the bits of tin, the scattered
glass, pin money, sheet metal
(scissored and shivery) of lakes,
precisely wild.

Domesticated men, who do not burn,
but inch and pound out lives,
yell to low heaven!
I am above it all.

2. On Insight

Wool over eyes, soft
over shine, the clouds begin to take
the edge off thought, the froth appearing
walkable and near, its grey
a density admitting no exception.
Now the ship of specialists begins
to sink, my high ideas go under—
feet lap heart neck head
in the clouds, in the blind
white folded deep.

3. On Time

We come through the ceiling
on dimmer wings. Streets widen,
paved with rain. The brown pull's
inescapable. We touch down, I give
up. I belong

in your house, in your arms,
in my own right mind. You'll fill me
with children, make me grave.

I say yes, let's get
down to it, let the dark itself

be why we're saved.

Inside

In the field is a house
of wood. A window of the house
contains the field.

You can't see far
with a sun in the sky,
with a living-room lamp

at night. Locality is all
you light, and you, as single
as a bed. But there's

no end to dark. The bed is in the clearing
and the clearing's in the wind; the world is a world
among others. Now your cell-stars split.

Form

We were wrong to think
form a frame, a still
shot of the late
beloved, or the pot thrown
around water. We wanted
to hold what we had.

But the clay contains
the breaking, and the man
is dead—the scrapbook
has him—and the form of life
is a motion. So from all this
sadness, the bed being touched,

the mirror being filled,
we learn what carrying on
is for. We move, we are moved.
It runs in the family.
For the life of us
we cannot stand to stay.

Syllables

The island doesn't sink.
It's not a ship, or spirits.
Doesn't try to keep up.
Doesn't care.
This comforts the lonely man.
He thinks like them
he's given up the ghost of likeness,
line and clause. But all along
the shoals of mated shapes
the boats will prowl and grind
and run aground. It's really farther out that his

survival finds its form: where
small and fat and striped
and never to be touched, they sing
their whole notes (heard or not)—
their boy low lub bob bell.

The Nymph to Narcissus

Si non se noverit . . .—Ovid

We invented one
another, the way water

and air are intimate,
the way reflection
is a lonely art.
If you're smart
you know better
ways to suffer,
know yourself
insufferable.
Is this true?
Is this true?

It was for beauty
that we did each other in.
You longed for no one,
I was reduced to doubletalk.
This is no way to live.

Of course I turned to
nothing but bones and a voice,
then nothing but voice.
Of course you couldn't stand
the sight, your ground. In love

the secret is the self; in death
the echo of the secret.

When the Future Is Black

Maybe it's our nature to be naming
the degrees of color, times of heat.
I love you, and we're up in arms,

a shotgun wedding
where the present
is designed to keep

the past and future from forever
meeting. So the woman, calling
herself alone, expects to die like that;

and the man, who calls himself together,
goes from one state of affairs to the next,
thinking them discrete

like colors or decades made
to wheel, like destinations
made to map. Alive or dead, we make

a world of difference. Or so we say
as, over our heads, the sky turns
blue to red in a space of minutes.

Message at Sunset for Bishop Berkeley

How could nothing turn so gold?
You say my eyelid shuts the sky;
in solid dark I see stars
as perforations, loneliness
as blues, what isn't
as a heavy weight, what is
as nothing if it's not ephemeral.

But still the winter world
could turn your corneas to ice.
Let sense be made. The summer sun
will drive its splinters straight
into your brain. Let sense be made.
I'm saying vision isn't insight,
buried at last in the first
person's eye. You

should see it: the sky
is really something.

Breath

What I want from God, feared to be
unlovable, is none of the body's
business, nasty lunches
of blood and host, and none

of the yes-man networks,
neural, capillary or electric.
No little histories recited
in the temple, in the neck and wrist.

I want the heavy air,
unhymned, uncyclical,
the deep kiss—absence's.
I want to be rid of men,

who seem friendly but die,
and rid of my studies
wired for sound. I want
the space in which all names

for worship sink away,
and earth recedes to silver
vanishing, the point
at which we can forget

our history of longing
and become
his great blue breath,
his ghost and only song.

Poems from To the Quick

(1981–1987)

Four Poems after Rilke

My friend, I must leave you.
Do you want to see
the place on a map?
It's a black dot.

Inside myself, if things
all go as planned, it will
become a point of rose
in the greenest land.

*

The fruit is heavier to bear
than flowers seem to be.
But that's a lover talking,
not a tree.

*

His eye-holes are empty. He utters
a word of correspondence and
dry silence bears the muffled sound
of a fertility, a flood.

Does he arouse or arrest it?
Who is in control—the magician himself?
A fatal fact could be conceived to finish off
such callings-forth, such holdings-back.

A word's an act, and no one can recover it.
Sometimes the thing we name
suddenly becomes . . . what? A being, almost
human, that the very calling kills.

*

It was from Adam's side
that Eve was drawn.
But when her life is done
where does she go to die?

Will Adam be her tomb?
When she needs that repose
will there be any room
in a man so closed?

The Amenities

I owe you an explanation.
My first memory isn't your own
of an empty box. My babyhood cabinets held
a countlessness of cakes, my backyard
rotted into apple glut, windfalls of
money-tree, mouthfuls of fib.

At puberty I liked the locks,
I was the one who made them fast.
The yelling in our hallways was about
lost money, or lost love, but not
lost life. Or so I see it now:
in those days I romanticized
a risk (I thought I'd die
in the alcoholic automobile, die
at the hands of nerveless dentistry). Small hearts
were printed in the checkbook; when my parents called me
dear, they meant expensive.

Where were you in all that time? Out looking for
your father's body? Making for your mother's room?
I got my A's in English, civics,
sweetness and light; you got black eyes, and F's,
and nowhere fast. By 1967 when we met
(if you could call it making an acquaintance,
rape) I was a mal-adjusted gush, a sucker for
placebos. Walking home from Central Square, I came to have
the good girl's petty dread: the woman

to whose yard you dragged me might
detect us, and be furious. More than anything else
I wanted no one mad at me. (Propriety,
or was it property, I thought
to guard: myself I gave away.)

And as for you, you had the shakes,
were barely seventeen yourself, too raw
to get it up (I said don't be afraid,

afraid of what might happen if you failed).
And afterwards, in one of those moments
it's hard to tell (funny from fatal) you did
a terrible civility: you told me

thanks. I'll never forget
that moment all my life.
It wasn't until then, as you
were sheathing it to run,

I saw the knife.

In a World of Taking, the Mistake

Down and down into your own regard
you double, dangling a bucket,
to take a shine. What's the secret?
You're not interested in anything

there's only one of. So the mirror is
amazing, and you find yourself inside it
to be deep. If you had another
fifty years, you'd feel no less

this wonderment at being—
framed in a standstill, your head
in the clouds (your likeness in mind),
you'd fall in love with reason. This

is the mistake. You think too much
of your life, far from oceans, far
from rivers, far from streaming. You think,
death I could bear, if it's anything like

this self in the calm of a held pail.
But the catch in the clarity comes then.
To look like this, you mustn't ever
be touched or moved again . . .

Two Loves

The backhoe braces itself against itself
with two flat feet, and fights
its appetite—I love that

shovel undermining just
the *terra firma* which its hinder parts
rely on. So the man in me

is making inroads everywhere (great cities rise
where he has wrecked the gardens)
while the woman in me

counterbalances his head-strong ways
by staying her ground, with equal force.
The latitudes of play

are ampler for the rules;
the clouds look clearer in a lake than not;
did poets live this long to practise

birth control? Excited by a simile, they take
the indecorum of a stagnant ditch, and make
a mirror of it. Meanwhile it's

the backhoe man who reads. At lunch he hunches
over his Inquirer, which is full of
spiritual facts of life, like

MALE GIRL GETS SELF PREGNANT, and he loves it.

The Trouble with "In"

In English, we're in trouble.
Love's a place
we fall into, so
sooner or later they ask

How deep? Time's a measure
of extent, so sooner or later
they ask How long? We keep
some comforters inside a box,
the heart inside a chest,

but still it's there the trouble with the dark
accumulates the most. The end of life
is said to be
a boat to a tropic,
good or bad. The suitor wants
to size up what he's getting into, so he gets
her measurements. But how much

is enough? The best man cannot
help him out—he's given to his own
uncomfortable cummerbund. Inside the mirror,
several bridesmaids look
and look, in the worst
half-light,

too long, too little, not enough alike.
And who can stand to be
made up for good? And who can face
being adored? I swear

there is no frame
that I would keep you in.
I didn't love a shape
and later find you fit it—
every day your sight was a surprise.
You made my taste, made sense,
made eyes. But when you set me up

in high esteem, I was a star
that's bound, in time,
to fall. The bound's
the sorrow of the song.
I loved you to no end,
and when you said "So far,"
I knew the idiom: it meant So long.

Spot in Space and Time

Despite his name, the dog's
an imposition—lying in the kitchen,
begging in the bedroom, with his lousy posture and unseemly
salivation—even Pavlov's dog exposes us (for men are known
by companies they keep). At least a dog cannot

expose himself—thank God it takes
some clothing to do that.

*

The chicken in its coop,
the chicken in its roasting pan, the chicken
in its place, I mean, with ruffles
of parsley at its ankles, doesn't seem
indecent. Then you sit it up
on the edge of a table and
cross its legs and look:
it's naked.

*

The indignant have a word
they cannot say alone: here (here).
The soothers say: there (there).
The dog's confused. He's neither

fish nor fowl. There in the mirror is
another dog, a fury of frequencies hackled.
Nor can Rover go to Esalen and
find himself; he scowls instead into the new
communications dish.

*

Remember how you dropped
that barbecued rib in your lap,
that casual affair in eighty-eight,
when everyone wore white?
Remember how the girls were all
named Faith and Prudence then? Today

the supermarket carts are full
of little Harmonies and Heathers.
Virtue's gotten mild, to say
the least. That's pretty
good, the mother says, that's
pretty pretty. Grandma falls
asleep, and there, in the deepest
doghouse, is a child.

*

Between the looking forward and
remembering, it's hard to find
a moment for the present.
I remember space from when
it was a nothing. Now we understand it's full,
with very little room for vacancy.
The latest on the emptiness
was on the radio: what's not,
said scientists, is smaller than we thought.
(Perhaps it is the thought

they're measuring, since
everything we know must fit
inside the temples where
a sky, by God, is understandable. It isn't nothing
we cannot imagine—nothing is the very stuff
of faith. It's *something*

we've forgotten, something
we are missing, in our human
grade and groove.) The thinker stands still,

thinking of himself, while (there, in his
abandoned microscope)
a million mountains move.

I Knew I'd Sing

A few sashay, a few finagle.
Some make whoopee, some
make good. But most make
diddly-squat. I tell you this

is what I love about
America—the words it puts
in my mouth, the mouth where once
my mother rubbed

a word away with soap. The word
was *cunt*. She stuck that bar
of family-size in there
until there was no hole to speak of,

so she hoped. But still
I'm full of it—the cunt,
the prick, short u, short i,
the words that stood

for her and him. I loved the thing
they must have done, the love they must
have made, to make
an example of me. After my lunch of Ivory I said

vagina for a day or two, but knew
from that day forth which word
struck home like sex itself. I knew
when I was big I'd sing

a song in praise of cunt—I'd want
to keep my word, the one with teeth in it.
Forevermore (and even after I was raised) I swore

nothing—but nothing—would be beneath me.

Constructive

You take a rock, your hand is hard.
You raise your eyes, and there's a pair
of small beloveds, caught in pails.
The monocle and eyepatch correspond.

You take a glove, your hand is soft.
The ocean floor was done
in lizardskin. Around a log or snag
the surface currents run

like lumber about a knot. A boat
is bent to sea—we favor the medium
we're in, our shape's
around us. It takes time.

At night, the bed alive, what
teller of truth could tell
the two apart? Lover, beloved,
hope is command. Your hand

is given, when you take a hand.

To God or Man

A line's not meant to lie there, longing
to be thralled into a coil. Give me a spike

in my EKG. The moment's meant
to jump, the moon returns, the drumhouse rolls us

all around. Send down a lassoist
or flute. And though it means

some truck with death,
(to whom I know

the spoils belong) I need
a shipment of your special fruit,

a flatbed of your basic seed.
In this, the country of

the angel and the witch (the underworld
a shadow of above), I see

at most and least a wing, I miss the long
and short of love. I've sent

this message out as many nights
as Zeno said it takes

to add the half-lives up.
The river holds the sky and yet

they move. (Where does
the blue begin? You needn't

answer in a word or flash—the water stays
and still the wave comes in . . .)

Bear in English

The animal *is* the act, the keeper says.
He's read his Yeats. He has
a PhD in Zen, and he has fixed
the communist flamingos with
his pinking shears. He's given all the monkeys
mirrors and allowances. I'm told

to play the sax like mad—a crowd adores
the blues.
                    But where are others like myself,
who feel the heaviness of human names—the weight
of withers, muzzle, rib cage, balls? Are bodies only
what the keeper says—a little occupation
for the mind? At night a hundred brilliant

parallelograms slide through my sleeping-room,
unhampered by the humped domestications I was once
so taken with. On Sundays,
consolation gets
dished out
(like, "Nothing actually
exists"). A slave is given
everything a slave could need—his gravy and
his glasses, lumps to love and roofs to look up to.
The keeper says this is the life! It never snows,
it never rains! But Christ, without a sky, I can't

have faith. I studied every day for years
(between the acts) to learn
his words for free, for once,
for all. But in his sentences were only two
varieties of voice, their premises the same.
They need each other, overlord and
underdog, and I became him,
as the mink became his wife. I mean

eventually language turned
into my only

way to know.
I found the words

and what they said
was "Do not let me go."

Animal Song

The fox knows many things, but the porcupine
knows one big thing.—Archilochus

We're flattered they come so close,
amused when they resemble us,
amazed when they do not.
The animal we named the sex fiend for
has no known family but ours. The angels, on the
other hand, can be identified by something
birds in any small backyard are largely
made of. If we do not move

perhaps they will approach us, in the spirit of
unearthing something. Everywhere inside the ground
are avenues and townships of another world,
enormously minute. And when we harbor
some largesse—a blue sky
no one knows where starts or stops—
then for a moment we don't terrify the animals.
It's rare, but it can happen. Someday, when the something

greater than our lives has come,
perhaps we'll stop our digging
little definitions for a hole.
Perhaps we shall recall
the language in which we were intimate—
before the literati, and before the fall,
before we called the creature names.
We'd have to talk with it, remembering

animal comes from soul, and
not the opposite.

Take Care

When a man dies, it's not only of his disease;
he dies of his whole life. —*Charles Péguy*

Our neighbor Laura Foley used to love
to tell us, every spring when we returned
from work in richer provinces, the season's
roster of disease, bereavement, loss. And all
her stars were ill, and all her ailments worth
detailing. We were young, and getting up
into the world; we feigned a gracious
interest when she spoke, but did
a wicked slew of imitations, out
of earshot. Finally her bitterness drove off
even such listeners as we, and one by one the winters nailed
more cold into her house, until the decade crippled her,
and she was dead. Her presence had been
tiresome, cheerless, negative, and there was little
range or generosity in anything she said. But now that I

have lost my certainty, and spent my spirit in a waste
of one romance, I think enumerations have their place,
descriptive of what keeps on
keeping on. For dying's nothing
simple, single. And the records of the odd
demises (stone inside an organ, obstacles to brook,
a pump that stops, some cells that won't,
the fevers making mockeries of lust)
are signatures of lively
interest: they presuppose
the life to lose. And if the love of life's
an art, and art is difficult, then we
were less than laymen at it (easy come
is all the layman knows). I mean that maybe
Laura Foley loved life more, who kept
so keen an eye on how it goes.

What Could Hold Us

Hats divide generally into three classes: offensive hats, defensive hats, and shrapnel.—Katharine Whitehorn

i

There are no accidents, or so
the lucky like to say.
In the department store she ran
smack into the clutches of
an unassuming man, and double-breasted them.
She drew away at once, but saw
he looked aghast at being
implicated so—with his offending
hands in air—they never meant
to take such liberties—and all around

stood mannequins, unmoved,
in shades of innocence,
in underwear.

ii

In the togetherness department, stores
leave much to be desired. The couches seem malposed
beside the barbecues, the bicycles beside the bras,
the customers beside
themselves, or reasonable
facsimiles.

iii

She hauled the bedroom suite to the public dump
where one man's paid to stay all day
and oversee the afterlife of wealth. She saw
what trucks and trunks delivered:
headless dolls, dead televisions,
tangles of forgetful lamp, a signmaker's
unwanted ampersands. And over everything

the dump man passed, with mercy and
a yellow *machina* (it's he
who parts the earth, who heals the wound,

who tends the jilted and who calms the dead). She stood there
by the empty pickup while he dozed

the king-size thing and earth together,
burning and the bed.

iv

However big the pain, the earth
can take it. Habeas corpus,
the raincoat wraps
the flasher's trouble up.
Habits close about the nun's
uncustomary hurt. The earth's big headache
(having so many of us in mind) is soothed
by a pacifist sky, with a bright blue sash,
or a few white flags, or a green
forgiving rain—whatever suits

the hidden haberdasher . . .

Point of Origin

They feed me and feed me and feed me
till the last
passions of the airport parting
are as far away

as any other earth. The cruelties, the furies of
recrimination (which is love) will pass.
In a minute, it's an hour ago.

Varieties of cloud go by,
varieties of blue. There's always
sun somewhere,
a clear to swear by, and I do.

*

Because we argued to the very ramp,
because I was the last to board,
because a man of many years

(nobody knew his language)
occupied my given seat,
I get to go first class.
A present! And the presents multiply, till soon

I am mistaking luck for privilege—I taste
a couple of lunches, have my little weep
in private, take a glass of wine
to make abstractions of, in geometric
ports of light. But all the while

behind me there, where calm
cannot be bought, where I was meant
to stay—somebody's baby cries
and cries and cries, impossible to pacify.

To the Quick

We fixed the ages of the irises at flower,
stopped the eons of the oranges at fruit.
Ripe was ready, since we liked to eat,
and beautiful was full by virtue of
the ear-eye-nose-and-throat man.
Time was sometimes said
to be at hand.

But not for a second
did the plant stand still.
The space we designated blooming—
where did it begin? The beans turned white
to green, and green to brown, and then
were no less Phaseolus; flesh
fell off into enormous
gravity, and seeds
were an end in themselves, in a way. On top

of the TV set I put
the baby pictures, meant to keep
the little person as he was, as still
as he could be. O man, o child,
we loved each other less

for how we moved
than how we stayed.
But what did we adore about the river?
Its unfixed address, and vagaries of bed.

Bar and Grill

The world the window held
was stirred—itself
was liquid, thickened slightly
toward the ground, where fast

pedestrians were passing by
and busses struck from silver mints
and bicycles well-spoken, and the host
of esses, nesses, motion making

individuals abstract, as motion will;
and then the window bound them
to the ground a bit, it
warped and rippled them, it drew them out—

however reticent the tucked dress was, it had
to bleed a little down; however pinned to stripe the suit,
it spilled an eyelet in the eyecup of
the bar and grill I saw them from.
Is this unclear? I was attracted

to the glasses there, some full
of purple corked, some pure
unstoppered mud, and all
about what disappears.
Whoever leaves

revises his
steadfaster's eyes.
You will not see me any more, that's why

the world cannot stop moving.

A Physics

When you get down to it, Earth
has our own great ranges
of feeling—Rocky, Smoky, Blue—
and a heart that can melt stones.

The still pools fill with sky,
as if aloof, and we have eyes
for all of this—and more, for Earth's
reminding moon. We too are ruled

by such attractions—spun and swaddled,
rocked and lent a light. We run
our clocks on wheels, our trains
on time. But all the while we want

to love each other endlessly—not only for
a hundred years, not only six feet up and down.
We want the suns and moons of silver
in ourselves, not only counted coins in a cup. The whole

idea of love was not to fall. And neither was
the whole idea of God. We put him well
above ourselves, because we meant,
in time, to measure up.

Big Ideas Among Earthlings

Who'd want to be the biggest one,
the president or mastermind—
the lord of stars, or model of
the kind? Who'd want the drove

of sycophants, the plague
of elitists and angels, echoing
her every word? A little
loam and nightsoil

is a lot. The miles unfurl
inside a single iris, small hours
in hot purple, wet gotten
from eavesdropping.

    *

We craved our own lost halves
ever since language and land
were sundered into kind.
And Africa misses

South America, and clouds
their coast. To this day I do love
the fucker who deserted me, but who can claim
to hold a soul—even her own? Americans think big

is forceful, but the strongest force belongs
to the electrons (bound, at 40,000 mph, about
their far-off nuclei); from them we get our sense
that matter's solid. You look

about, above, for lords and kings. But given
what we know of strangeness, given what we know of charm,
perhaps the god is small, not big,
who keeps us from harm.

Or Else

In memoriam: Mitchell Toney

What could we say to you
while you died? Could we
say "we"? Could we say "stay"?
(Who, after all, was moving?) My life was always

dealing in words, but now I'd better
listen, shut up and listen,
by the ditch of silver,
by the uninvested moon—all night among

the wealth of speechless
elements (where unlit earth
is dumbest): listen

for the shiver of a sign. Or else you die as surely
to, as from, us.

The Ghost

I held my breath for years, for fear
of being breathless, fear of being
afraid. Whenever someone left my bed
I took a deeper one. Addicted

to the flesh, attracted to the very quick,
I thought I'd never
let them go (my child,
my man, my love of home). But lately,

in the winter stoneyards,
when the still heaps
hold their blue, and a hand is all
wool thumbs, and no one says

hello, or hello's other half,
and stars, above all, after all,
strike fire from the lapidary slope—
then something rises

out of me at last—my hope
and heat, the spirit I
had trusted most. We have to give up

everything of love—
even the ghost.

What Poems Are For

They aren't for everything.
I better swallow this, or else
wind up shut up by openness so utter.
Nip and tuck, poems are for

a bit, a patch, a mended
hem, carnation's cage—and then
the heart may bloom, the sex may roar, the moment
widen to be the well the child

fell in forever—yes—but not until
I've checked the pinafore
and laced the meat,
puttied the stones, and pinched

the flowers back. I can't give you
a word to hold the dead. I can't give you a name
to hold a god, a big enough denomination. Find yourself

a church instead, where roofs are all allusions
to the sky, and words are all
incorrigible. Timelessness, and time,

they are not mine to give. I have
a spoon, a bed,
a pen, a hat.
The poem
is for something,
and the world is small.

I'll give you that.

The Matter Over

It is better to say "I am suffering" than to say
"this landscape is ugly."—Simone Weil

From the piling's kelp I drew
the starfish with its five blunt fingers.

First I thought the creature
less than handsome—less of a hand

than I expected: rigid, with a stumpy gray
asymmetry of grasp. It wasn't soft. It hardly moved. So maybe

it was dead? I couldn't see
beyond myself, until I turned

the matter over, and beheld
a host of unfamiliar

facts: minute transparent
footlets, feelers, stems

all waving to the quick, and then
the five large radials beginning

gradually to flail
in my slow sight and then,

in my thin air, to drown.
I'd meant

to send it
as a gift to you

who were my missing part,
so far inland. Instead,

to a world the sighted
have no rights to, to the dark that's out of mind,

I made myself resign it,
flinging the hand from my hand.

Poems from Shades

(1981–1988)

Mox Nox

"Ultima Multis" means "the last, for many."
Like it, "Mox Nox" ("soon, the night") and
every other expression translated to form this
poem were found as inscriptions on sundials in
the Hautes-Pyrénées.

Hasten slowly, the sundial said.
Day and die are cast together.

Covering, I discover
said the dial. All things are dream.

They fly as you stand still.
You may know hours

but you do not know your hour:
light is shed

but the last
is hidden.

Shade warns shade
(the sundial said).

20-200 on 747

There is rain on the glass but it all disappears
when I look toward the curve on the world.
(The here and now is clear, I mean, so we
can't see it.) Given an airplane, chance

encounters always ask, So what
are your poems about? They're about
their business, and their father's business, and their
monkey's uncle, they're about

how nothing is about, they're not
about about. This answer drives them
back to the snack-tray every time.
Phil Fenstermacher, for example, turns up

perfectly clear in my memory, perfectly attentive to
his Vache Qui Rit, that saddest cheese. And now an interlude,
    while we
commiserate: it takes what might be years to open
life's array of incidental

parcels—mysteries
of red strips, tips and strings, the tricks
of tampons, lips of band-aids, perforated notches on
detergent boxes, spatial reasoning milk-carton quiz and subtle

teleologies of toilet paper. Mister
Fenstermacher is relieved
to fill his mind with the immediate
and masterable challenge of the cheese

after his brief and chastening foray
into the social arts. We part
before we part; indeed,
we part before we meet. I sense

the French philosophers nearby.
I hope not in the cockpit (undermining
meaning as they do, or testing aerial translation's
three degrees). They think

we're sunk, we're sunk, in our little
container, our story
of starting and stopping. Just
whose story is this anyway? Out of my mind

whose words emerge? Is there a self the self
surpasses? (Look at your glasses, someone
whispers. Maybe the world
is speckled by

your carelessness and not its nature.
Look at your glasses, if you want
to see.) Who says? We're not
alone. The town down there

grows huge; one tiny runway
will engulf us. Is the whisperer
Phil Fenstermacher, getting a last word in
before the craft alights? I look

at my glasses. I see what he means.
They're a sight.

What Hell Is

March 1985

Your father waits inside
his spacious kitchen;
he himself is corpulent,
and powerless. Nobody seems to know exactly
how your illness spreads; it came
from love, or some
such place. Your father's bought,

with forty years of fast talk, door to door,
this fancy house you've come home now to die in.
Let me tell you what hell is, he turns to me:
I got this double fridge, all full of food,
and I can't let
my son go in.

　　*

Your parents' friends
stop visiting. You are a damper on
their spirits. Every day you feel

more cold (no human being here can bear
the thought—it's growing huge as you
grow thin). Ain't it a bitch, you joke, this

getting old? I'm not sure I should laugh;
no human being helps, except
(suddenly, simply)

Jesus. Him
you hold.

　　*

We're not allowed to touch you
if you weep or bleed.
Applying salve to sores that cannot heal
your brother wears a rubber glove.
With equal meaning, cold or kiss
could kill you. Now what do I mean
by love?

*

The man who used
to love his looks
is sunk in bone
and looking out.

Framed by immunities
of telephone and lamp
his mouth is shut,
his eyes are dark.

While we discuss despair
he *is* it, somewhere
in the house. Increasingly
he's spoken of, not

with. In kitchen
conferences, we come
to terms that we can
bear. But where

is he? In hell,
which is the living room.
In hell, which has
an easy chair.

Unspeakable

While he was dying of
everything, inside and out,
I caught in dreams at night some kind of

scale or bark that spread across
my face and arms until I looked
diseased myself, and knew myself at last:

and found no peace in knowledge, after all.
My friend by contrast
I presumed to love

beyond the physical (beyond the dream)
and as he got cadaverous and sore
it made me more

devoted than I ever was
in all the days of his untrammelled
vanity. Easy for me

to love while he lost hope,
to dream while he lost face,
while he began

to undergo again
that painfully unfinished state
a child is made to suffer—

body that won't stay put or known, its visage
ranging and deranging, and its self, at best, at twelve,
tufted with fresh atrocities of hair. Adults

forget, but not for good.
My friend stopped talking, wrote
a final poem, having shit for subject

and last word. His sister said
his lips turned inside out. The heart
keeps drumming and

drumming it in but still
I do not understand. What's
dead? What's dead?

*

With eyes in our heads,
we are not made
to see ourselves. Instead

the hundred people
packed inside this flimsy tent
look out for something

wildly unfamiliar—thrilling
to organs and candy and banners, agog
for antics of a circus animal (the town

is small, the winter long; we've craved
exotic incarnation, trains to swing
or sway us, fancy women, or a man

miraculous). Instead we get
this painful elephant, put
through his paces

on a red footstool,
playing the fumbling footman or
terrible tuba, playing the fool; and all around him

hoots and titters start to swell toward
full-blown derision, and I'll tell
you why: thanks

to a bad road diet, and confinement,
and his shitty life, the elephant
is defecating now, voluminously, out his

nether end (how *could* he, everybody gasps)
while waving
daintily, in front,

the scarf, coquettish, meant
to make him cute. He lumbers and revolves,
saluting everyone, this way and that; what he can't see

is half the show: and half the audience, by turns,
is treated to the sight
of how the stuff emerges,

where it lands. The snickers
are the language of
the animal the animal offends,

the one that thinks
it's different. We can't
contain ourselves: the laughs

burst out in spatters from the stands . . .

Inflation

Language wasn't any
funny money I was playing with,
no toy surprise, no watch or wooden
nickel, not
a nickel nickel, either,
twice removed, sign of a sign.

I meant to make
so deep a song
it held no end of love.
But now I'm dumb

to frame the stream
of stills I feel,
stuck in the onrush without any
one that I was singing to,
without a you, while currents go on running up
a bill of silver senselessness—the seconds counted

in the hundreds, in the thousands, in the billions, till the till

is bust. Remember how enormous
one old swollen moment
used to be? Remember how we loved

position 99, the one where you
look forward? Man, as I
look back, I wonder how

did numb get so comparative?
How did the verb to come

(our childhood's bright
infinitive) become

so narrow a necessity?

The Lyricist's Lament

I never learned the trick of snaps, got sick
on canapes and wit, could never open up

somebody else's rented suit to find
the real gorilla underneath. I missed

the point of alligator shoes,
odd monikers and utter individuals,

and even Lulu Obligata's last soirée
was lost on me. Within an hour I could see

constituent millenia but not a second,
in myself a whole society but not

a single you. (We lyricists are like
to stay home typing up

the sub-groups of the lyric self, beloved
admiral of all our mirrors.) Maybe this

is love asleep, love slumming, love
where sub- and object cannot be

distinguished, love in which it's just
too easy being true.

The Oven Loves the TV Set

Stuck on the fridge, our favorite pin-up girl
is anorexic. On the radio we have a riff

of Muzak sax, and on the mind
a self-help book. We sprawl all evening, all

alone, in the unraised ranch;
all day the company we kept

kept on incorporating. As for the world
of poverty, we did our best, thanks

to a fund of Christian feeling
and mementos from

Amelia, the foster child, who has
the rags and seven photogenic sisters we prefer

in someone to be saved. She's proof
Americans have got a heart

to go with all that happy
acumen you read about. We're known to love

a million little prettinesses,
decency, and ribbons on

the cockapoo. (But who
will study alphabets for hands? Who gives

a damn what patience goes into
a good wheelchair? Who lugs the rice

from its umpteen stores
to the ends of the earth, to even

one dead-end? Not we.)
Our constitutional pursuit

is happiness, i.e.
somebody nice, and not

too fat, we can have
for our personal friend.

Who Made Her

She is half who made her. —*Wallace Stevens*

You put the house about my body,
stud by stud and space by space,
till it seemed all the frame
a freedom needed,

twelve stars in a window more
than any universe at large.
You made room in the world for me,
four rooms, to be

exact, the number
of chambers made
to beat.

     *

So screw good manners—
there's no nice
prim syntax for
the baby's loss—the wailing comes

as utter unbecoming,
pain from brainpan,
rocks from voicebox,
sex from the confessional, my god

how could you disappear?

     *

In Chinese scrolls the lovers curl
around each other for
millenia. And babies

are forever being made
with perfect little parents in their cells.
A carpenter constructs a house of hope

inside the house of pine. Mine too, I thought
the joiner's art. But now I see
my song has issued

never from the cool remove—no love
of each thing in its place, no bed or bank
against the rushes, nothing toward

about a boat, no where or way
to steer it. Lord, you
made me, made me, made me

goes the song (but can we bear to hear it,
all that blame and praise inseparable?).
I loved you more

in throes than theory,
in spasms than in spirit.

Earthmoving Malediction

Bulldoze the bed where we made love,
bulldoze the goddamn room.
Let rubble be our evidence
and wreck our home.

I can't give touching up by inches,
can't give beating up
by heart. So set
the comforter on fire and turn the dirt

to some advantage—palaces of
pigweed, treasuries of turd. The fist
will vindicate the hand; the tooth
and nail refuse to burn, and I

must not look back, as
Mrs. Lot was named for such
a little—something
in a cemetery,

or a man. Bulldoze the coupled
ploys away, the cute exclusives
in the social mall. We dwell

on earth, where beds are brown,
where swoops are fell. Bulldoze
it all, up to the pearly gates:

if paradise comes down
there is no other hell.

Hole Filler

The cat is killed
by the passionate petter,
the poem by clappers
who mob its best-laid calms,
and looks are eaten up entirely
by beloveds, apples no one wanted once

the worm had had his fill. From
happiness and hurt in equal
parts, the lovers cry; as
for the gigolo, he has
an eye for what?
An eye.

ID

Did I? Is it?
Hit below the belt, the ego

doesn't know the difference,
KO, OK, ego can't

identify its problem, can't
identify itself. O cogito,

it says, O sum.
And then, in its cape,

freed from the pay phone, who
says "I have come," and in the name

of whom? Somebody's
living in here, deep inside, but still

the elevator's stuck, the clock
is slow, the news is yellow

in the hallway stack. The ego's
middle name is mud. There's trouble in 4A and now

there's trouble in 2B; the plumbing
leaks, a hole is in the head, and tell me

how did all this happen?
Is the super dead?

To Have To

is an odd infinitive, in which
compulsion and possession meet
and share a word together.

Both propose, and both accept;
to have, because it wants to hold;
have to, because it has no will.

But then there is
no past or present, either:
coming's going, in this match.

It's odd because they're two at one
but endless, in the end, in their
capacity to be attached . . .

Not a Sin

It's not a virtue either, really, this
rubbing and rubbing against someone, yourself
a someone too, until

someone must burst or yell. It falls
where pleasure and necessity and risk
all intersect—we have ourselves and
to ourselves, to love and half
to death—removing, move
by move, the overlays of mind until

we're down to sheer medulla.—Not
what you would call intelligent, and yet
I bet it has some wisdom in it, something
that can bear us later, past
the lapse in gushes, past
the businesses apart, past weeks
and decades made to keep
our waking lives on line until

the moment comes no telling knows to welcome, and
no wording comprehends, reducing all
our big ideas to
jolts of oblongata, ah

my underestimated God, shall I
show forth thy praise? You made
my powers crash. As bushes burst,
as flames float off in heart-boats,
in the flood, I open up
my mouth and find
you've filled it full
of flesh. I mean

you made me feel
the way I feel
so words would not
be proud. I know.
You made men so I'd kneel.

Spilled

The waiter dropped a tray of glassware and
the din of conversation stopped as if
in shock at competition. Not
until that moment were we
quite aware

of what a roar
the ordinary made—not till a knife of
other noise could cut right through it
to the greater emptiness, to zero, there

where no one for a moment
said a blessed word. And then
the nothings started
coming back, the hum
of small talk re-arising
gradually to flow and
circulate again, its rhythms
welling up out of the hole in the story
to make the story normal once again,
the cruise control back on,
the life as a career
in which we can afford,
as usual, to fail to hear.

*

This restaurant's a dressing up of selves
in dreamy twos and fours. Their fantasies
are being fed, their livings made.
These hundred couples can, tonight, pretend

they are accustomed to such cooks and maids and then,
by some consensual agreement (because none
can really be the monarch of the model) must ignore
the commonplace proximities, the many

foreign monarchies that eat their fill
nearby. We make do with

a little privacy, say three by two, and make
believe we're different. The dream is purchased

at the price
of never seeing being
from above, or from a distance, somewhere
difference might disappear. And all

of what is being said, in this packed room, and all the other
rooms on earth, might add up to a single animal's
identifying cry—flung far
on waves of ether, waves

of ESP. For all we know
that's how a God is reached, in whose
bright synaesthesias of sympathy a blood
need not be red, if spilled as speech . . .

Hard

Suppose you have
to move a mountain.
Do you call up All-or-Nothing Limited
with blasters in battalions, and dispatch
the under- and the other-worldly
straight to smithereens?

A moment blows
what several thousand years could ease—
time moves the planet all the time without
demolishing the delicate—no opposition
between powers, no antipathy
of east to west. The networks go

so far and fine we can't
conceive them—intricacies of a single
rock or river, rate of rainbow—look!
I can't get over it. Let all your big
bulldozing eras
snore their fast Manhattans down;

let lovers of the good and quick
erect their clever rocks (the graveyard has
its own downtown). Let book-ends wind up being all
our reason for the books, and men learn only yes and no
in other people's languages, believe no code but cracked
(perhaps their wills need
execution often). I

have harder work to do,
a teardrop at a time, until

the whole world's stoneworks soften.

Melted Money

Time and time again we told them
not to leave their stuff so near the stove.
But children have no past, and so
they don't believe in futures, really.
Whiles and whiles of smoke unwind

from houses, causing
more or less sky, I
can't tell. I spent
my life forgetting how
a music can be made to pour
right off the measured page,
and intuition flood the calendar.
But animals go stitching our
enumerated yards together, world
already without end. A little

gold spills out from windows
in the neighborhood (has everybody spent
too much on God's next birthday?). Thanks
to the invisible, we are alive. Take heat: you can't

directly see it, but it spins a shadow, clear as any
cast by iron stove. It is the meaning
of the stove, and moving off from it. The children now are

nowhere to be seen. The children's pictures look
undone. And soon the flesh-colored crayons begin
to melt into earth-colored ones . . .

Stairwell

The telescope's a microscope,
the stars are in our eyes, and not
all orders come from somewhere
you could call above.

Rivers of money, streams of time,
the current has its twists of DNA.
When terminals permit, you feel
the future move. What makes us dead

can make a rail alive. I swear it was
a wisdom in the dream that said
(after the priests and politicians left
the pulpit) its piece. It spoke like nothing

in an ordinary story, wasn't anyone I knew, it had
no context, not a pitch or tempo, but it kept
insisting "Death is
in a second." I thought, that's just

great, another *carpe diem* dream, and it
lashed back at me, "No! Listen! Death
is in a second, IN, it's *in*." It meant,
I gradually gathered, death's inside—

not only soon, but now, deep down,
where space and time are
not to ends. (Despite the boundaries
between named states and naming men,

no God is nailed to knowledge—that's
the trouble with the tree—no wise is nailed
to where, no way to when.) That hint was all
the dead can give. Since then I've dreamed

non-stop: there is no other way to live.

Labor

Each sword of the plant is burning.
You would not believe
what surgery midwinter light
can do, cutting

subject from object. I don't want
the way I used to, rushing to have
and swallow whole. Death takes
its time; little by little

I've lost my taste for victory.
Let others fight for rank and class.
I pass. It's better
plants and stars

prevail without our interloping,
eyes for certitude and arms for love,
our pens for poor taxonomies, our
campaign promises and rant. Too long has love

been taken for belonging—
let it, with its banners, fall away. I have
to carry water now; I need
to feed the plant.

The Typewriter's the Kind

for Raya

The typewriter's the kind
of heavy gray that's rare these days,
and good for leaning on. I sit
in front of it, with holes

torn in my meanings, or a heart
so full of complication I can't even
start to start. And on
the radio the cello's

unaccompanied, and on the hour
the news is *entendu*. I lay my arms
upon the typewriter, my head
upon my arms, and breathe and
breathe and breathe, and there

is all the cool
immutability a fevered
human needs, its current humming constant like

the speed of light or fact
of water (there is death
on earth this moment, there

is death on earth this moment . . . Always

is already). Then
I can get up, and go about
my work, which is to love to see

the endless world's unsavability.

Place Where Things Got

I always thought if I could just
remember where I started, I
could understand the end.
The cat upon my lap

infolds itself, intends itself;
it makes itself a compact
package, perfectly adapted to
the transient circumstance of my repose.
It chooses, out of live adjacency,
best balance in the fewest gestures,
all intelligence, no thought.
It wraps the rest
around itself, and settles.

For a time its engine runs
continuous, it bumbles and
it hums and drones, and then
slows down, so little

interludes of stiller stuff occur, some
quietude in patches, here and there, and then
another strength of hum crops up, to just
drop off, drop

deep and deeper in
to dream, to stir, to dream,
till only

little nubs of noise arise, the
intermittent particles of purr . . .

*

When moments hadn't melted into ages yet
my sister Jan and I

conducted sound experiments at night
in our shared room. We ground the parts
of sentences down past
a word to syllables,

past syllables to
letters, letters
into even less.
The grindstone was
the voice's own
slow-motion: if you spoke
in strictest graduality the
symbol turned to substance,
meaning broke down into means.
Beginning atomists, we shifted
rpm until the noise was gravel,
and the gravel grain, and then

the particles themselves became distinct.
In exquisitely slowed-down utterance you found
the sands inside a saying, molecules like what
a cartoon Superman is made of,
held up close. The grown-ups

wouldn't tell us
what is *in* a loaf of time or life
of story, what's *inside* a voice, in other words—
not counting what the English teachers wanted and not
    counting
what the weary took for granted—what's *in* there, aside
from coins of meaning? That is why

we took the trail of crumbs ourselves, broke breadstuff down,
backtracked from mines of money toward the mill
where dough turned into seed and seed to cell and there
(beyond iotas of the minuscule) we found

a place where things got huge again.

Round Time

Looking back, I look
too straight: I can't locate
my old self, I mean young self,

you know who. My one-and-only,
be-all-end-all, my intended and my ex, the one I was
most smitten with. No matter in how many

shots and tones and letters she
was caught, recorded, dated,
lovingly held still or held

important, now
behind the frozen frame she stays
essentially unrememberable—not to be

surrounded, comprehended—even in time,
or *especially* in time. And if I try
to ride the wave without

desire for destination, just
remembering remembering's
design—the feedback

slaps me silly, still, with
multiples of ism, replicas of ness—a busy copy center,
Lake Success, with mirrors posed for turns, returns,
    diminishing . . .

We *are* what we are looking for: a sign.

        *

My fingers cannot tell themselves
from the electric typewriter. The room
rises and falls in mind, the bay beyond the window
has its day, whose islands are the islands of
attention. What exists is mostly
lost on us, and this

despite our best intentions,
fastest memories. As quickly as
this cat leaps up upon the desk to
settle on the manuscript—a curve

will overcome the line.

Shades

The day shines down in waves
and particles. The Sunday patrons
of the open-air café are shimmering—
their eyelids, earlobes, orbits all
isosceles-bespangled.

Over obligato streams
of car-sparkle arise
the brilliant disquisitions of
the fork on plate. Here is a baby's whoop
for brief on human happiness, and there
(above the five-and-dime, against
an empty blue—or is it just
the eye that's uninhabited?) the pure

line of a spire. What more could we want
than this world, sharpened
by shine and dark, faceted
by accident, anchored by
appearance? Well, we could want

the dead to be with us again,
be with us still, be *somehow*
undiminished (somehow unbegun), so we
won't die the way we fear. They could
be here, in all the carnivals of cups and trade,
with faces chance might turn to ours,
in sympathy, in mirrored shades . . .

But no. The world makes
too much of itself. No sense allowed
beyond the few and five: it's blinding, deafening,
demanding and alive. A thousand diamonds splinter out
from fender, windshield, chrome—a spray of glints,
a glance of blades. The human being, struck, can just
put darker glasses on.

Thought of Night

Just think of it, and you
surround it with

its opposite. That's thought's
domain. Take here

and now, for instance.
Do we see a line where there

is none? We draw
up sides, forgetting how in cells

division made things whole. To me
I'm complete, but I'm partial to you.

*

So as we fall
into the night (which isn't,

after all is said and done,
the opposite of day) I cannot see

our differences. Love mends
the broken language. We are each

the first of persons (though I know
I mustn't speak for two). I only mean

I feel myself again,
and it is you.

From 20,000 Feet

The cloud formation looks
like banks of rock from here,
though rock and cloud are thought

so opposite. Earth's underlying nature
might be likeness—likeness
everywhere disguised

by wave-length, amplitude and frequency.
(If we got far enough away, could we
decipher the design?) From here

so much goes by
too fast or slow for sight.
(Is death a stretch of time in which

a life is just a flash?) Whatever
we may think, we only
think that we will lose. The foetus,

expert at attachment,
didn't dream that
cramped canal would open

into sound and light and love—
it clung. It didn't care. The future
looked like death to it, from there.

Acknowledgments

Many poems from my previous books were first published in magazines and anthologies, which are acknowledged here:

From *Dangers* (Houghton Mifflin Co., 1977):
   Harper's Magazine: "Excerpt from an Argument with Enthusiasts, Concerning Inspiration," "Solitary's Solace in the Natural Sciences" (under the title "Spinster Discourses on the Natural Sciences").
   The New Yorker: "It is 70 degrees in late November. Opening a window, you nearly know," "Spectacles."
   American Poetry Review: "Against a Dark Field."
   Seneca Review: "Pupil."
   Antioch Review: "Ozone," "The Score" (under the title "Playing the Numbers").
   Antaeus: "Double Agent."

From *A World of Difference* (Houghton Mifflin, 1981):
   American Poetry Review: "Hag," "High Jinx."
   Aspen Leaves: "Breath," "Whoosh."
   Green House: "At a Loss" (under the title "Pro Quo").
   Hudson River Review: "When the Future Is Black."
   Moons and Lion Tailes: "The Nymph to Narcissus."
   MSS: "The Fall" (under the title "The Meaning of Fall"), "The Field."
   The New Yorker: "Toward an Understanding" (under the title "On Time").
   Paris Review: "North Island Songs," "Inside."
   Ploughshares: "Message at Sunset for Bishop Berkeley."
   Poetry: "Mind."
   Poetry Miscellany: "The House."
   Virginia Quarterly Review: "Impressionist."

From *To the Quick* (Wesleyan University Press, 1987):
   Poems from the book first appeared in the following magazines: *The American Poetry Review, Antaeus, The Atlantic, Harvard Magazine, Kayak, The New Republic, The Paris Review, Science 84, Seneca Review, Tendril.*
   Some of the poems also appeared in anthologies: *The Antaeus Anthology; The Generation of 2000: Contemporary American Poets; The Morrow Anthology of Younger American Poets; New American Poets of the 80's; The Norton Introduction to Literature.*

From *Shades* (Wesleyan University Press, 1988):
   Poems from the book first appeared in the following magazines:

Boston Review, Exquisite Corpse, Harvard Magazine, Michigan Quarterly Review, Painted Bride Quarterly, Sonora Review, Threepenny Review.

Poems also appeared in the following anthologies: *New American Poets of the 80's; The Norton Introduction to Literature.*

Among the new poems in *Hinge & Sign*, the following appeared in journals and anthologies:

"Dry Time," "Some Kind of Pine," and "Two St. Petersburgs" in *Jacaranda Review.*

"Tornado Survivor" in *Gargoyle* and *Editor's Choice* (Spirit That Moves Us Press).

"Glimpse of Main Event" and "Amniotic" in *Agni Review.*

"Place Where Things Got" in the *Godine Anthology of Contemporary American Poetry.*

"The Mirror" in *The Journal.*

"What He Thought" in *Tikkun.*

"Scenes from a Death" in *Western Humanities Review.*

"Well" (under the title "Intensive Care") in *Boston Review* and, as part of a much longer poem, in *How(ever).*

"Numberless," "The Woman Who Laughed on Calvary," and "Connubial" in *Iowa Review.*

"Window: Thing as Participle," "Untitled (there is much unsaid)," and "Sound Mind and Roses" in *Virginia Quarterly Review.*

"Acts of God (Lightning)" in *The Cresset* (Valparaiso University).

"A Hurricane Can Cast" and "Coming" in *The American Voice.*

"To Go," "For a Sad God," and "The Song Calls the Star Little" in *The Eloquent Edge.*

"Better or Worse" (under the title "Nothing I Foresaw") and "For A Man" in *Decade.*

"What Hell Is," "By Faith Not Sight," and "Third Person Neuter" in *Poets for Life: Seventy-Six Poets Respond to AIDS* (ed. Michael Klein, Persea Books, New York, 1992).

The series "32 Adults" grew out of a collaborative project with artist Tom Phillips, whose collages provoked this quiltwork of pieces. They first appeared in a 1990 edition by Richard Minsky (New York) and the Talfourd Press (London), under the title *Where Are They Now?*

I owe debts of thanks and affection to those who have given me encouragement and support over the past twenty-five years: my parents; my brother and sister; Gregory Biss; Kurt Biss and Raya Garbousova (my second parents); Ellen Bryant Voigt and all the writers I've known at the MFA Program for Writers (originally at Goddard College and now at Warren Wilson College); also extraordinary colleagues at the MFA Writing Program at the University of Washington in Seattle, the Writers' Workshop in Iowa, Syracuse University, U.C. Berkeley and Irvine, and a host of lively programs I've visited around the country. As honorary godmother to Bryan Gardner, I've enjoyed an extraordinary friendship for fourteen years now; his good spirits and affection have meant more to me than I can say.

Grants from the following endowments made possible some of my most undistracted times of teaching and writing—the Guggenheim Foundation, the National Endowment for the Arts, and the Lila Wallace/Reader's Digest Program administered by the Woodrow Wilson Foundation. I've been uncommonly lucky in such editors as Jonathan Galassi and Terry Cochran—and luckiest of all in quality and constancy of companionship, in the person of my husband Niko.

HEATHER McHUGH is Milliman Distinguished Writer-in-Residence and Professor of English at the University of Washington in Seattle. She regularly teaches at the low residency MFA Program at Warren Wilson College, near Asheville, NC. She is the author of six books of poetry, including *The Father of the Predicaments* (Wesleyan 1999), *Shades* (Wesleyan 1988), *To the Quick* (Wesleyan 1987), *A World of Difference* (Houghton Mifflin 1981), and *Dangers* (Houghton Mifflin 1977). In 1993, Wesleyan published her literary essays, *Broken English: Poetry and Partiality*. She has translated three volumes of poetry: *Glottal Stop: 101 Poems by Paul Celan* (Wesleyan 2000), translated by McHugh and her husband Nikolai Popov, *Because the Sea is Black: Poems by Blaga Dimitrova* (Wesleyan 1989), with co-translator Popov, and *D'Aprés Tout: Poems by Jean Follain* (Princeton 1982). Her version of Euripides' *Cyclops* (with an introduction by David Konstan) is forthcoming in a new series from Oxford University Press. In 1999, she was elected a chancellor of the Academy of American Poets.

LIBRARY OF CONGRESS CATALOGING-IN-PUBLICATION DATA
McHugh, Heather, 1948–
    Hinge & sign : poems 1968–1993 / Heather McHugh.
      p.   cm. — (Wesleyan poetry)
    ISBN 0–8195–2213–9. — ISBN 0–8195–1216–8 (pbk.)
    I. Title. II. Title: Hinge and sign. III. Series.
PS3563.A311614H56   1994
811'.54—dc20
                                            93–35917